REPORT FROM PART TWO

GWENDOLYN BROOKS

Third World Press ● Chicago

REPORT FROM PART TWO
by Gwendolyn Brooks

First Printing, 1996. Third World Press, Chicago

Library of Congress Catalog Card Number: 96-83057
ISBN 0-88378-162-X (paper)
ISBN 0-88378-164-6 (cloth)

All requests for reprint permissions are to be referred to:

Gwendolyn Brooks
P.O. Box 19355
Chicago, Illinois 60619

REPORT FROM PART TWO

GRATEFUL ACKNOWLEDGEMENTS TO:

The David Company, Broadside Press, Third World Press, Harper and Brothers, Harper and Row, Humanities Magazine (The National Endowment For The Humanities), DrumVoices Review, Beloit Poetry Journal, Lands End, Tri-Quarterly, The Chicago Tribune.

REPORT FROM PART TWO

CONTENTS

BASIC INFLUENCES	1 0
KEZIAH	2 1
IN GHANA	4 4
BLACK WOMAN IN RUSSIA	5 3
THE DAY OF THE GWENDOLYN	7 6
FAMILY PICTURES	122
"I'M HERE"	144
APPENDIX	161

Afterword by D.H. Melhem   **146**

BASIC INFLUENCES

BASIC INFLUENCES

PARENTS
BOOKS
CHURCH
MOVIES

PARENTS. From Report From Part One: Home always warmly awaited us. Welcoming, endorsing. Home meant a quick-walking, careful, duty-loving, never-surly mother, who had been a schoolteacher, who played the piano, sang in a high soprano, and wrote music to which I wrote the words, made fudge, made cocoa and prune whip and apricot pie, drew tidy cows and trees and expert houses with chimneys and chimney smoke, who helped her children with arithmetic homework. Home meant my father, a janitor for McKinley Music Company. He had kind eyes, songs, and tense recitations for my brother and myself. We never tired of his stories and story poems. My father seemed to Gwendolyn and Raymond a figure of Power. He had those rich Artistic Abilities, but he had more. He could fix anything that broke or stopped. He could build long-lasting fires in the ancient furnace below. He could paint the house, inside and out, and could white-wash the basement. He could spread the American Flag in wide loud clean magic across the front of our house on the Fourth of July and on Declaration Day. He could chuckle. No one has ever had, no one will ever have, a chuckle exactly like my father's. It was gentle, it was warmly happy, it was heavyish but not hard. It was secure and seemed to us an assistant to the Power that registered with his children, always, as magic. My father, too, was almost our family doctor. We had Dr. Carter, of course, precise and semi-twinkly and efficient--but it was not always necessary to call him. My father had wanted to be a doctor. Thwarted after one year's training, he read every "doctor book" he could reach, learning fine secrets and curing us with steams, and fruit compotes, and dexterous rubs, and, above all, with bedside compassion. "Well, there, young lady! How's that throat now? Well, let's see. This salve will take care of that bruise! Now, we're going to be <u>all right</u>." In illness there was an advantage: the invalid was royalty for the run of the seizure.

MAMA! --telling me when I showed her, at seven, a page of rhymes: "You're going to be the lady Paul Laurence Dunbar!" Star-bits in her eyes! She and my father praised me to anyone who visited the house. And my mother praised me to Langston Hughes. She made me show my poems to him when he came to recite at our church, Metropolitan Community Church in Chicago. And she praised me to James Weldon Johnson, author of "God's Trombones," when he came to a *fancier* church: her assault was-- "SHE'S the one who sent you all those wonderful poems." The great Dr. Johnson drew himself up, which he had every right to do, crossed his hands in front of him. "I get so many OF them, you kno-OW," was

11

his textured response. Our encounter with Langston, though, was comfortable, regenerative. "You're very talented!" he exclaimed. "Keep writing! Some day you'll have a book published!"

BOOKS. My own Book Story begins with my father's wedding gift to my mother. He gave her a bookcase. Dark, dark mahogany. Departmental. It was (is) rich with desk, drawers, glass, friendly knobs. And it was filled with -- The Harvard Classics! I shall never forget visiting it as a little girl -- over and over selecting this and that dark green, gold-lettered volume for spellbound study. Oh, those miracles. Nine Greek Dramas. Adam Smith's "Wealth of Nations." Emerson's "Essays and English Traits." Locke, Hume. Darwin's "Origin of Species." Franklin, Woolman, Penn. Pilgrim's Progress, Donne, Herbert. White white white. I inherited these white treasures. (My brother died in 1974.) Bookcase and books are in the southwest corner of my bedroom.

The Harvard Classics were not our only transports. We had other reading matter in the house. We had all of Paul Laurence Dunbar's books, from which my father read to us, in the evening, after dinner. We had a famous Black magazine, "The Crisis." We had "Liberty," and "Up From Slavery." We had a wondrous, large, red English cartoon book, "Wit and Humor." -- which I've lost. We had collections of medical books -- in which I loved to dip. We had art, too. We had volumes of art, much valued by my brother Raymond, who wanted to be a painter, and who was genuinely talented. Raymond and I, coming home from school!--- to cocoa and cookies, and a mother eager to hear of our homework, and brightly ready to help us conquer it. Oh, those autumn-trips downtown to the Textbook Store! -- to buy our own copies of our schoolbooks-that-had-to-remain-in-school. Sping-spang new were the copies we bought. Our OWN COPIES. Delightful to look at and to hold. *Ours.* Both Mama and Papa were determined that we should have those books at the beginning of each autumn, for our very own. (Sacrifices were made; happily.) Ownership of those textbooks made us eager to handle them, eager to study. What fun it was, to rove among the aisles of that Textbook Store, inhaling the fragrance of brand new books, watching Mama make those purchases, and leaving the store a little reluctantly -- with our so-special new possessions.

AND! _____as soon as we were old enough, our mother saw to it that we had library cards to the Forrestville Branch Library. The Forrestville Branch was Enchantment-land. I was allowed to check out four or five books at a time. In a few days I'd bring them back, and take out more.

SOMETIMES WE VISITED <u>THE DOWNTOWN LIBRARY</u>! The DOWNTOWN LIBRARY now contains Sara Miller's bronze interpretation of me -- staring across the room at

Saul Bellow. Just the two of us. What do we say to each other when the library is closed?

Home and library taught me that books are bandages and voyages. Links to light. Keys and hammers. Ripe redeemers. Dials and bells and healing hallelujah.

CHURCH. "Beulah At Church," one of my poems for children, in an early book called "Bronzeville Boys and Girls," carefully describes how I felt about church in those early church-going years.

> You have to be just clean, you know.
> You have to be just straight.
> No door-screen dust upon your nose.
> No rust from the iron grate.
>
> No rust, either, from the fire-tongs,
> with which you may like to play.
> And you should not be loud at all,
> Nor even very merry;
>
> But only hold your song-book — so! —
> With the big people closing you in.
> And the organ-sound and the sermon,
> Washing you clean of sin.

I do not want to stay away.
I do not think I should.
Something there surprises me:
It feels good to be good.

Of course, later I wrote "The Preacher: Ruminates Behind
The Sermon." That poem has been banned in a number of
places.

MOVIES. A truly horrible thing was that I grew up to
womanhood and went through early womanhood believing
that the glittering white family life on the screen *should*
be my model.

I understand so well, now, the way I felt *then*, the way
other Blacks felt *then*, about seeing Black people on the
screen. In those old years, when Blacks crept into the
story, we shrank from them. Instinctively we knew they
had No Chance. Most movie-going Blacks, in those times,
were not exposed to the sentience of a W.E.B. DuBois or a
Chancellor Williams (he wrote "The Destruction of Black
Civilization") -- although there was such: most of us did
not know of any Malcolm-type wisdom to instruct us off
our knees -- although there was such. But we had, at
least, the muted sense to comprehend the gist of film-
maker messages. They were as follows: "Blacks are

laughable. Blacks are ridiculous. Blacks are, by nature, subservient. In movieland, you are not to shake hands with Blacks. You may pat them, if they're good, somewhere on or above the head. Seldom may you allow yourself, your white self, the expense of gazing, human-to-human, into those negligible eyes." What, NEVER? Well, hardly evER. (Thanks, Gilbert and Sullivan.)

We Black patrons sat in the dark. In the dark we Black patrons stared at the screen. There they were. (Occasionally.) On the screen. Those intruding COLORED folks! (one of the stupid names we then called ourselves and allowed ourselves to be called.) Those NEGROES! Those intruding would-be stars! Those negligibles, those masters of stumble-English. Bug-eyed, pop-mouthed, endlessly terrified, endlessly loyal to whites (on the screen, at least), endlessly disloyal to and suspicious of other Blacks: ---- not to be trusted, not to be respected, guaranteed --- not to be thought of seriously. Those folks were the Interrupters. They came onto Our screen, Our wonderful, clean, elegant white-folks screen, Interrupting personal Escape, Interrupting personal white-oriented Dream, (which dream, of course, was unreal "even" for whites.) If those interlopers, those Interrupters, were not there, we Black patrons could feel whole, could THINK we felt whole. in the sweet lulling dark of the theatre, we could feel we were part of The Great Life, could MOVE: had a CHANCE. Secretly, we were ashamed of Those

Black Folks up there: we felt their love for money exceeded their pride.

THEN! -- with seeming suddenness, we were in the Sixties! My own first movie startlement was Sydney Poitier's "The Lost Man." It was not a successful picture. We were approximately new at this "Strong Black" business. The picture fumbled. It went forward, then backward. It stuttered. And, of course, we had to be served with the ho-hum cliché of the Black man roughly stepping on and over the love and warm resistance of a Black woman to reach a rich Liberal-type Caucasian girl. BUT. I remember my own breathless excitement and pulsing pride when I saw, for the first time in my life, a solid screenful of hot-willed, stone-eyed Blacks, moving sharply, with raw strength and deliberate prudent anger. Of course, they failed. CAREFULLY. Nevertheless I, and other Blacks, left the theatre with an exhilarated notion that a Statement had been made. "Buck and the Preacher." by the way, was a completely successful and an integritous Black picture. Interestingly, it was directed by Poitier and Belafonte. Blacks therein were presented as complex, reasonable human beings, capable of warm-heartedness, justified indignation, capable of courage, coordination, organization, subtle humor, and Black man-Black woman love, deep and sweet. Rather than shuffles, eye-bug and soprano timorousness. Blacks were presented as capable of achieving what they set out to do. Blacks truly loved this picture. They felt large as they looked at it. Many saw it two or three times. I went to see it three times, and I am a fan of its TV presentations.

Accompanying movies, sometimes, was--VAUDEVILLE! Downtown and at the South Side's Regal Theatre. There would be Duke Ellington and Ella Fitzgerald and the likes of Cab Calloway and Ivy Anderson and Snake-hips, of course. But Otherwise, the fact of vaudeville, TOO, might tend toward tension! --in the white theatre, that is.

DOWNTOWN VAUDEVILLE

What was not pleasant was the hush that coughed
When the Negro clown came on the stage and doffed
His broken hat. The hush, first. Then the soft

Concatenation of delight and lift,
And loud. The decked dismissal of his gift,
The sugared hoot and hauteur. Then, the rift

Where is magnificent, heirloom, and deft
Leer at a Negro to the right, or left____
So joined to personal bleach, and so bereft:

Finding if that is locked, is bowed, or proud.
And what That is at all, spotting the crowd.

WELL! My Basic Influences. What, today, is their condition?

I rarely go to church. My religion is kindness.

My parents are dead. But they are my models still. Their instruction and their love continue. In seventy-seven years and five months I have encountered no models superior to them. AND I have met three presidents and a Queen. (Netherlands).

Today, my movie-going is meager. But if my TV offers Buck and the Preacher, Boyz n the Hood, Twelve Angry Men, The Good Earth, Amadeus, Babette's Feast, Fiddler on the Roof, James Joyce's The Dead, Jesus Christ Superstar, A Passage to India, Frank Gilroy's The Subject Was Roses, or Spike Lee's Malcolm X, I attend. I use VCR, but my daughter, Nora Brooks Blakely (brilliant), or my husband, Henry Blakely (brilliant), must set it up for me.

BOOKS! (Again!) Books invite and entrance me still. I still love their insides and their outsides. I love to flip off their paper jackets to experience their bindings.

I - BUY - BOOKS.

Many are sent to me by editors, many are given to me by friends. Never mind: I - BUY - BOOKS.

Startled indeed was a bookseller in Whitefish, Wisconsin. Before my reading in that town I scurried into this nice bookstore with roomy red leather chairs all through it, "just" to look around. The bookseller couldn't BELIEVE that this old Black woman in mundane clothing and what people like to call my bandanna   was buying almost $300 worth of books. (Via credit card, of course.) There was an inquisition. "Are you buying these books for a <u>library</u>?" No. "Are you buying these books for your <u>employer</u>?" (He was just decent enough not to say "Your Lady.") No. "Are you buying these books for _____" "Look," I interrupted -- pleasantly -- "<u>I</u> <u>like</u> to <u>read</u>." He looked at me as though I had said "I like to climb to the top of Mount Everest." Indeed, I believe **that**   announcement would have made more sense to him.

Note: National Book Award Medal acceptance speech on November 16, 1994, New York.

KEZIAH

On Tuesday, March 14, 1978, at eight in the evening, two weeks after her ninetieth birthday, my mother stopped.

Keziah Corinne Wims Brooks.

She had been healthy most of her life. She had been a fast walker, a joyously rhythmic little walker, most of her life. Most mornings, her waking was with pleasure in the new prospects, pleasure in new planning. She was an alert contributor to the procedures of her milieu.

In 1976 she had published, happily, her book of memories, her impressions, with a couple of fictions. She had insisted on calling it "The Voice, and Other Short Stories." She had insisted on paying for its publication, out of her own savings. I gave her an autographing party at Chicago's South Side Community Art Center. Many attended, many spoke in tribute to her. Her last sister, Beulah, came from Topeka to assist her. Seven hundred fifty dollars' worth of her books were sold! She gave a speech, reading it with precise distinctness, precise delight. (I remembered that, a few years earlier she had given an impressive speech at a Metropolitan Community Church celebration in a downtown hotel with no paper in front of her, amazing the throng with her self-possession and soft dignity.) At this party, she enjoyed the refreshments, the piano music, the flowers. And there was a wide big-lettered banner across the gallery:

CONGRATULATIONS, MRS. KEZIAH BROOKS!

Ke-ZI-ah. I have always loved my mother's name. ("Corinne" she had given to herself.) And I love her nickname, "Kip", which, strangely, she didn't care for.

There had been that strange sorrow of losing her only son, my brother Raymond, in 1974. But that sorrow did not prove flattening; it was not such as could persuade her to Resign; Hoke Norris' Chicago Sun-Times article on her reported her as saying she didn't have "a worry in the world!" --- this, at the age of eighty-nine. Interestingly and sadly, by the time that article appeared, on January 22, 1978, Hoke, novelist and Sun-Times book editor, had died, and my mother saw it, rather hazily, in the hospital. I taped it to the wall above her narrow bed at Michael Reese. The Michael Reese doctors and nurses were impressed.

There had been the Robbery. <u>That</u> was <u>almost</u> flattening. That happened on a particularly joyous Sunday morning in the spring of 1977. My husband and I had taken her to a nice restaurant for brunch, after a grocery-shopping trip. I remember her very special happiness. She couldn't praise, enough, the food which she ate with such delight, nor the attractiveness of the room; nor my "kindness", as she chose to call it, in taking her on the financed shopping trip, although this was an almost regular happening. After the little festivity -- she considered restaurant visits singular specialties -- we took her home. As a rule, my husband, on arrival at her door, would see her into and through the house. But on this occasion, because I was leaving, immediately, for the airport, with just enough time to make my plane, he saw her through the door only. A couple of hours after my arrival at the campus I'd flown to, my agent called, with the news that my mother's home had been robbed, during our brunch absence -- robbed of all those articles a thief can sell easily: phonograph, radio, television set, electric fans, etc. I called my mother. By that time, my husband had "secured" her with a repaired and barred back door and dining room door. She was dazed. Such a violation! To think! Strangers moving around in Her House, handling Her things! She couldn't get over it! The police were called. They apprehended no one, although neighbors told us it had been the work of three brothers on the block, three brothers who subsequently went to jail for another robbery in the area.

Invasion. She couldn't get over it.

She never did get over it. We spelled her decline from the moment of that invasion. It wasn't long before she began to lose interest in food. Although very slender all her life, she had loved food, selecting it, cooking it, daintily eating the products of the recipes she had collected over the years. But after the invasion, I might return from a lecture trip, laden with gift groceries, and find no evidence that anything had been eaten since my departure. I would find only the little gray-green sculptured cup, from which she liked to drink water, on the kitchen sink. The ice box would seem undisturbed.

"Aren't you eating, Mama?"

"Yes, I'm eating."

"Well, I went to Stop and Shop and got you some wonderful lamb chops."

"Oh, thank you!"

But she got thinner and thinner.

Then one Sunday in October something happened that alarmed her as well as ourselves. I had told her I'd go to church with her that Sunday. Always, on such an occasion, she would be charmingly dressed and at the window watching for us, waiting. This time, I had to ring the doorbell, then knock knock knock at the door, and at the vacant window, repeatedly, before attracting her attention. Finally she came to the door in her nightgown and robe. She seemed bewildered, but when I mentioned church, and told her that Henry was in the car, ready to drive us down, she suddenly remembered what she had entirely forgotten. She was abject, contrite. She couldn't forgive herself. She began immediately to "collect" herself, and in no time she was neat and ready to go. Yet, nothing like that had ever happened before, and she was truly alarmed.

That was the last Sunday she ever went to church.

Something else disturbed us. Always willing to be chatty, always responsive to what others had to say, -- she had always listened attentively to the ideas and opinions of others, and had responded with eager liveliness -- she became increasingly silent.

I asked her, over and over, to live with me. My house was about thirty blocks south of hers. I told her I would expand my five-room cottage, so that she could have her own quarters, her privacy. She wouldn't come. She loved her home. She wanted to live alone. She had stopped renting out her second floor, because she wanted "peace and quiet." Once, during this time, her furnace, tampered with by one of those professional tamperers, one of those roving "furnace-fixers" I had warned her against, exploded. Fortunately, my husband and I were visiting her at the time. It was a very cold winter night. We bundled her up and insisted, of course, that she come to our house, until I could get a new furnace installed in her basement.

I'll never forget her poignant "I <u>wish</u> I could stay home!" as we helped her down the snowy steps.

I had a new furnace installed, and she came back to her precious home. She proceeded with her steady decline. She ate less and less. Soon, she Wasn't Well. That is the way to put it. Yes, she was eighty-nine, but for Keziah Wims Brooks to be Not Well was <u>strange</u>.

Because, although she <u>was</u> weak and, finally, had to stay in bed, (except for going to the bathroom — two rooms and a rough road of strain away) — all we could observe, in the way of wrongness, was that she was not eating.

I moved in with her. I called the office of her doctor. Edward Beasley, a highly-respected pediatrician, was doctor to all of us. He had seen both my children through sniffles, measles and chickenpox. When, many years before, I had decided my heart was "failing", he had seen me through the fantasy. "He's dead," said a woman at the other end of the line. Very carefully, I gave my mother that news. "That's --shocking," she said, with precise quiet. She meant those words exactly. It was, as they say, "the end of an era."

I had to hunt up another doctor. Val Gray Ward told me that a Fred Daniels was willing to make house calls. Mama seemed to trust him. She allowed him to influence her into a neighborhood clinic, a clinic on 43rd Street near King Drive. She had told me she did not want to go to "any hospital." And she had written up a little document which stated "in no uncertain terms" (an old phrase of hers) that she wanted NO OPERATIONS. She was so weak on the day of her visit to the clinic that Henry had to carry her in. Dr. Daniels was able to convince her that she must go to a hospital for examination and treatment. She listened to him with polite concern. She looked at me, then, and said another poignancy -- "Well -- I'll just have to rely on your judgment."

Responsibility. I was, from that moment, entirely Responsible for my mother -- bills, care, chores, decisions.

She entered Michael Reese. A couple of days after she was settled in there I read to her a piece I had written on an Amtrak train . . . . Tuesday, November 29, 1977. Narrow in her narrow hospital bed, very still, she listened attentively to my assessment, clumsy and innocent (and criminally inadequate, as I later knew) of her voyages, her countries found. Then she said, with acceptance round and gentle, "That's nice."

I had always wanted a "simple" I-love-you from my mother. I do not remember any. I have no memory of volunteered motherly hugs and kisses in any department of our life together. In adulthood, I would hug her on arrivals and departures. She would respond with apparent pleasure and participation. But displays of affection were not spontaneous. (My own children I squeezed, kissed, grabbed on sudden impulse. Even when she was two, I was forever looping up my little daughter and carrying her from one end of the house to the other; she was almost like a doll; "Why don't you put that child down?" my husband would say.)

Yet my mother's affections, we all knew, were present and clear. As daughter, as sister, as mother, as wife, as grandmother, as neighborhood friend, she was subscriptive and serious and yielding.

After her death, I found in the treasured old desk she had inherited, from her brother Will, a notebook in which she had inscribed gift paragraphs to her eight inheritors. Her elegant handwriting! Nothing else was in that 10-1/2 inch by 8 inch fifty-sheet blue notebook, called by its commercial creators "<u>Sterling</u> Quality". My gift, "To Gwendolyn", was:

Dear Daughter, I am truly appreciative of your many kind deeds. They have given me much comfort and happiness. I hope your success continues and that you will be happy throughout life. Love, Mama.

I have never been one to put much stock in <u>dreams</u>. But --
how pleasingly marvelous it is that we see, after their
deaths, mother and father and brother, and sometimes
aunts and uncles, in our dreams. As <u>well</u> as the thousand-
and-three monsters and gargoyles and strangers charming
or wan! There they are, semi-coolly or warmly
wonderful; physiques, aspects, expressions very much as
usual. And INTERESTED in us.

So, I lost and shall never lose my Mother. She turns
up in dreams, again and again, her mother-eyes regarding
me. She says a few words; answers a question; or looks-
just looks.

Here is the testimonial I took to her in the hospital:

In a little poem I have written about my mother, I have
noted the particulars of her character. The poem
commends my mother's essential strength. Keziah
Corinne Wims Brooks was and is a courageous woman. It
has never occurred to her that she should slink away from
any of the challenges of life. The challenges of life -- the
agonies, sorrows, the million and ten frustrations,
perplexities, problems, reductions, dominations and
explosions -- <u>she</u> has looked at with a calculating eye, has
judged, has catalogued. She has tamed what had to be

tamed, what could, what should be tamed. She has adjusted to whatever rocks were super-ornery, determinedly smoothing the edges of such rocks so that she might sit <u>bearably</u> thereon. No fear, no fight, no fury has been so oppressive as to leave her weaponless. Even now, in her eighty-ninth year, when certain details of this New Time begin, shockingly, to seem unconquerable (home invasion, cruelty to the very old and the very young, our accelerating human coldness), she has thought of a way of redress: she is proceeding into the depths of herself, where it is warm and cozy, receptive, comfortable. From these depths, into which her friends cannot follow her, she waves with a genial pleasantness, but she says very little, and she will not let us pull her out. Withdrawal, then, is her Last Weapon. So far as <u>she</u> is concerned, it works. It is a resource that works.

This change in her - alarming to <u>us</u> - dates from October of 1977. The home invasion in the preceding spring had shaken her fundamentally. Her loved television set, a gift from her daughter, had been stolen, her doors splintered in the forced entry during, luckily, her absence. In October, her heating plant failed, and even though assured it would be replaced, somehow her faith in her ability to control her environment began to waver.

About the new silences (due partly, I think, to fear of forgetfulness and partly to a willingness to learn from the busytalk of others, and partly to I know not what) -- I am

reminded of some very wise lines of the Fugitivist poet
Merrill Moore:

> . . . . silence is not death.
> It merely means that the one who is conserving breath
> is not concerned with tattle and small

quips."

Poem:

My Mother
Of Keziah Corinne Wims Brooks;
Of yesterday's strength.

My mother sits in yesterday
and teeters toward today
and topples toward tomorrow's edge
and panics back away.

Yesterday taught her to contrive
to dreg-up and to thoroughlize.
-- Fitting her for Some reckonings
with the not-old and with surprise.

(December, 1975)

Yes, my mother, born March 1, 1888, is a daughter of
yesterday. She has always been, however, willing to
sally forth, albeit cautiously, to test or question today's
new thing, today's strange thing. She is even willing, as

I've implied here, to topple toward an exhilarating, tentative, almost mischievous little combat with the hints, science, promises, problems and affronts of tomorrow; but, her steady intelligence tells her, the waters of tomorrow are indeed too deep, too deep for her, and she "panics back away", leaving the larger risks of tomorrow for the solving hands of the young. Even so, she has certain lessons to hand down to the young -- certain positives that, she believes, were reliable yesterday, are reliable today, and will be reliable tomorrow unless we humankind are going to start from scratch with new gods, new earth, new sky, new exits and entrances, and an absolute revolution, or reversal of decisions. Yesterday taught my mother to go down to the very roots of things, the very roots of life, thoroughness, that dutiful calm determination to be Equal to this life, to this world that has made it possible for her to face -- cleanly, deliberately, reasonably -- with "innocent" and steady eyes -- whatever comes, whatever rises before her.

My mother 'brought up' my late brother Raymond and myself in the sunshine of certain rules. One: we must be clean of body; she scrubbed us vigorously until we children could satisfy her high standards of cleanliness. That was outside! As for cleanliness inside, long before it was fashionable to consider diet with strict seriousness she was so inclined. Our meals were healthful, inclusive, attractive, controlled. Two: we must be dutiful. Dutifulness has always been her major concept. "Always do the Right Thing." Three: we must empathize with other people. She was fond of quoting her own mother, Luvenia Wims -- "If you know yourself, you know other people." Four: We must respect ourselves. Our bodies were monuments of purity and beauty and we were not to poison them with filth of any kind, with disrespect of any kind. Our minds were clean and shining crystal, into which we were to pour only what was clean and bright and good. Five: we must respect the honor of Family -- in the smaller sense our Family of Four plus our scattered relatives-in-the-large (although she would not have expressed it in this way), our Family of the Black millions all over the world. We must put no disgrace on Family. Six: we must WORK for what we use and enjoy. To steal -- the merest match or marble or licorice switch -- unthinkable! Other people's property is sacredly theirs. (And, it follows, ours is sacredly ours.) Seven: we must be polite and helpful to other people. This meant each of us must meet all, friend, stranger, with a pleasant face; a nod, a salutation. This meant, until such behavior in Chicago became perilous, allowing the hungry unknown to sit at table; or giving a dollar here, a dollar there -- often ill-afforded. Eight: as long as we were children and controllable, we must go to church and respect God and Godliness. Godliness was a combination of decency, kindliness, and the observance of Duty.

These mother-charms -- abetted by my father's underwriting concern, protection, and reliable love -- are the good to which I continue referral, and which I consider my continuing nutrition.

Thank you, Mama.

KEZIAH'S HEALTH BOOK

(When she was eighty-eight, I asked her to write _another_ book, a tiny book of health suggestions and other aids for the old. I gave her a beautifully decorated blank book for this task and I think she created what follows with a kind of awed pleasure. On the first page is the general title "Articles and Paragraphs" -- which meant that she had intended to tackle other subjects too. Then come the health instructions under the title "Beneficial Health Habits." The entire ten pages are in her own beautiful script.)

Beneficial Health Habits

A long life is due to many good health habits. I have lived to be 88 and feel nearly as well as I did ten years ago.

One of my most important requisites has been an annual check-up by a responsible physician. My great concern is hypertension. Several of my relatives have had strokes so I deem it necessary to be extremely careful;

hence I am always supplied with high-blood-pressure medicine.

Eating proper food is my next important habit. I am so careful about eating and drinking things that are beneficial that a special diet is used daily. I drink a cup of hot water before breakfast, which consists of a dish of oatmeal and a glass of pineapple or orange juice.

My lunch is eaten about 4 hours after breakfast. At this stage of life, the less meat I eat, the better I feel, so I eat a very small amount of meat, preferably lamb, but occasionally a piece of chicken is a substitute. Since I find beef constipating, I avoid its use. I habitually have 1 or 2 meatless days a week. On these days I usually eat an egg. Since cooked eggs are constipating, I beat a raw egg and stir in 3/4 cup of milk, one teaspoon of honey and flavor it with a fourth-teaspoon of vanilla extract. This for me is non-constipating. It is a good substitute for meat and makes a palatable drink that all partakers will enjoy. During my lunch I also eat an average amount of stewed vegetables which I prepare by cooking string beans, celery, carrots, tomatoes and zucchini together with several cups of water until tender. This is a very healthful food so I prepare enough for a few days.

My dinner at six o'clock consists of a half cup of V-8, diluted with a little water, a dish of stewed fruit, a piece of toast and a glass of milk.

The things that are most detrimental to my health are nuts, pork in any form, sweets, fibrous food, seeds and skins, so I avoid the skins of fruits and vegetables, and never eat pork.

The only exercise I engage in is my housework, which I do without help. The exercise I get from shopping tours is sufficient for my limbs. I tried some of the exercises recommended by experts but soon discovered that too much exercise is worse than an insufficient amount. I always keep witch hazel on hand for massaging my limbs in case a daily task exceeds the normal amount of work I do.

Senior citizens should be very careful about the excessive use of their eyes since all parts of the body weaken with age. My sight was the first part to weaken. This happened at the age of forty. Before the morning of that memorable day my vision was seemingly perfect. I went to the porch for the newspaper. On reading a few lines of the first page I was surprised and dismayed to discover I could not read the fine print and would have to use glasses.

Another beneficial habit which some people neglect is to dress warmly in cold weather. A large percentage of pneumonia is caused by the lack of proper clothing. I often see bare-headed boys and men, with short hair, on the streets in cold weather, and wonder how they escape illness.

Another healthy habit to form is cheerfulness. Those who are around antagonists will find this characteristic hard to establish, but perseverance and a definite decision to let others have the last word will be well worth the effort.

Rest periods are predominantly important. A bed rest of one hour is perfect but if this amount cannot be arranged, a half hour is better than none at all. I learned from watching my mother that some tasks we ordinarily perform while standing, can be much more restful in a sitting position, such as using a stool at the sink while peeling potatoes, apples, etc. One can also sit at the board while ironing some of the weekly laundry.

During the last year of my husband's life, my stooping position for weeding my flower bed was relieved when he made a low stool for me by sawing off the legs of a high one, thus decreasing my tired feeling immensely.

When these helpful habits have been faithfully formed, supporters who escape accidents can expect long healthy lives.

My Afternote:

On "page 2", right after "and a glass of pineapple or orange juice" is a crossed-out passage, which went as follows -- "and a cup of tea. The beverage until recently was coffee. My decision to make the change was a desire for my life to be prolonged. I assumed that coffee could have the opposite effect."

Near the back of the book was a slip of paper on which she had tabulated her wordage per page. The total was 746 words.

Mama's ninetieth birthday morning, thank goodness, was cheerfully sunny.

On what was to be (two weeks later) her death bed, on what had been my father's death bed, in the second room of her house at 4332 Champlain Avenue (we called that room the living room, and the first room "the front room") she listened to me explain to her that I had brought her out of the hospital because I knew she wanted to be in her loved Home -- that I wanted her to be peaceful. She "latched on" to that last word. She said distinctly "I am peaceful." And she looked at me directly, cleanly, as though she wanted me not to doubt the gold of what she was about to say to me -- the gold contained in two words. "THANK YOU."

How carefully she said those words.

And I knew that "Thank you" was for everything, for all of my smilings, every embrace, every care, every Easter lily and Christmas poinsettia, every youthful achievement and childskip, every shopping trip and party-for-her, every box of chocolates, every introduction to a celebrity, every healthbook bought, and dress and coat and Stop and Shop lamb chop, for the trips to New York and California (she refused to accept my offer of a trip to Europe or Africa, although once she had said "When I'm ninety I'll go to Africa.")

<u>That</u> was the wholesome Thank You; the complete Thank You.

In the early afternoon, our old Champlain friends, Carter Temple friends, Ida DeBroe and Kayola Moore Williams, came for a birthday visit. Merry Kayola had been one of my first Sunday School teachers. (Indeed, I can remember, as Sunday School teachers, only Kayola and sweet-tempered, tall, moral Mrs. Ida Barnett.) I "grew up" with Ida DeBroe and her brothers and sister on Champlain Avenue. We sat near Mama's bed and gossiped about old times and present assignations. It delights me even now to remember my mother, weak as she was, softly chuckling and looking at us with suddenly brightened and mischievous eyes! Two weeks before she was to die, and at the age of ninety, she could "rise to" good, spicy, "naughty neighbor" stories!

Before they arrived, I had been playing the piano for her. Many of her favorites -- including a Carrie Jacobs-Bond piece. I played "Just A-Wearyin' For You," which all our family had always loved. I played "The Scarf Dance" by Chaminade, the only "classical" piece I knew by memory. Mama listened contentedly.

In the early evening we had her birthday party. I bought a special birthday table-covering and napkins, an exquisite cake, ice cream, candy, candles -- everything. Mrs. Flossie McGhee, whom I had employed to nurse my mother when I could not be there with her, helped me dress her in radiant finery and sit her at the dining room table. She stayed up perhaps half an hour, and seemed aware that we were celebrating a Milestone.

Naturally, my husband's camera, brought over for the occasion, did not "work;" I have no pictures of a scene most precious to me. I've hated myself for not pre-stocking the house with <u>five</u> cameras.

When everyone had gone except myself (Henry gone, Nora gone, Mrs. McGhee gone), I turned on television -- and there was <u>another</u> birthday present for my mother: Arthur Rubenstein was "in concert". She was able to enjoy some of her favorite music. She had always loved Arthur Rubenstein's piano-playing. Once, I had taken her to Orchestra Hall to hear him.

A last bow-ribbon on a very pretty day.

P.S.

Summer Sunday School picnics. I liked only the getting-ready: helping to make the peanut butter sandwiches, with crispy green lettuce, packing the fried chicken, the deviled eggs, looking at the white cake or coconut cake and devil's food cake with white icing.

Through the years I've had conflicting memories about our once-a-summer trips to Riverview (Amusement Park). Nice. Not nice. What I did not enjoy was being in such crowds. The only scary "ride" I ever went on was the Silver Flash. What I did enjoy was something Safe: the Merry-go-Round, which Mama and I shared every summer. And the high point of the excursion, so far as I was concerned, was lunchtime: hot dogs, popcorn, cotton candy, pop. (Lemonade?) Mama <u>seemed</u> to enjoy the whole day, although happy to come home in the twilight, Riverview "achieved" and packed away for another year.

IN GHANA

In the summer of 1974, I go, with my husband, to Ghana. Ghana, West Africa. I had visited, alone, East Africa's Nairobi, Kenya, and Dar es Salaam in Tanzania, the summer of 1971. Now to experience the cities of Accra and Kumasi in Ghana.

Henry is struck by the large-letter signs in the Accra airport: "Invest in Ghana!" "Incentives For Foreign Investment Are Numerous." "Resources For Industries Are Abundant." "Prospective Investors: You'll Gain By Investing In Ghana!"

The Ambassador is commodious, well-equipped, handsome. My many-colored anticipations that I would find huge bugs running around in the pretty little bathroom are never to be realized. The ceiling fan is more efficient than most air-conditioning I have known. Downstairs, the dining room is cool and cheery, and the food is tasty and pleasantly served by careful waiters.

When we step outdoors for our first get-acquainted-with-Ghana walk, we are immediately hailed by Bayour Ameru (pronounced By-or Ah-mer-oo.) "Hey, Ameri-cann!" Bayour has a car, and he wants to be our guide through Accra. For a fee. He is slender, a little under medium height, has that cool amiability, that non-intrusive matter-of-fact cordiality ideal in a guide. He is dryly self-confident. He is a BUSINESSman. And he seems to know everybody in town. As we are driven through the streets of Accra, we hear, over and over, "Hey, Bayour!" Smiles, smiles. He smiles back, or lifts an acknowledging hand. You yearn to understand the sources of this respect.

Bayour takes us to a huge department store, which looks and acts like any number of American huge department stores. I buy African dresses.

On Friday, Bayour takes us to a little West Indian gift shop, whose owner, a short tan woman, is delighted at the number of expensive purchases I make. I buy scarves, beads, a woven bag, a dashiki.

I take lots of popcorn and candy to a school, and distribute it to the delighted children. They call me "Mama." I cannot remember a thing about the school except the happiness and smiles of those beautiful children.

We are told that Accra is the cocoa capital of the world. Accra is the home of the National Museum, which we visit. It is rich with arts and crafts, many of which are thousands of years old. And we are impressed with the general revelation that here (it is true in the greater part of Africa) art and utility are one.

On Saturday, Bayour drives us to the zoo. Well, after my experience of the Nairobi game park, any zoo is -- just a zoo. But I do fall in love with the wonderful snakes -- enormous, calm, coolly coiling, exquisitely designed and "painted." In their deep abode, they look like huge jewelry.

We are taken to a Chinese restaurant. Then we go to a weaver's. I take a picture of the weaver. Seated on the bare floor, in a dull corner, scantily clad -- barefoot. His body busily involved with threads and rope and wood. His face intently still. He is <u>weaving</u> -- and that, apparently, is all that makes any sense in the whole world. I shall never forget that tight sight.

On this first Sunday, a good Sunday breakfast in the dining room of the Ambassador Hotel. Then we have a long walk to the ocean. It is "breathtakingly" beautiful out there on the beach. Fresh air, that seems different from <u>all</u> United States fresh air. Sunshine. Children playing. Men and women quietly strolling as they chatter (about what?)

On our walk back to the hotel we are interrupted by a long young man who tells us of his life of forlorn mischance, of active misery. Naturally, I press upon him a cedi. I am rebuked by my husband, who decides I've "been taken."

Back to lunch in the hotel dining room. Henry insists on making notes of the prices of everything we eat -- as he has done and is to do throughout the trip.

Cape Coast

Monday. Bayour Ameru drives us to the bus station. An exciting trip ahead. We have a two and a half hour drive on a beautiful modern bus to Cape Coast. There, a taxi to Elmina Castle:

The wet floors. The ancient, cruel walls. The death's-head above the barred iron door of the small dungeon in which hundreds of <u>difficult</u> slaves were put, to die. No windows, no water, no food. Because they were expected to die in three days. Most did. Those who somehow didn't oblige were taken out to have their throats slit. (The next-door dungeon was for a number of male slaves. Certain female slaves, the "comelier," were kept in a long court. These "specials" were sent up a long, secluded ladder, through a trap door, and into the Governor's quarters above, for gubernatorial use. When these women became pregnant, <u>they</u> were <u>freed</u>. "And the mulattoes you see in the town now," our guide informed us, "are the descendants of such white and Black 'union.'")

Oh that long hall, with two doors at the end, through which slaves were shipped out. Dozens of bats on the ceiling. We saw the kitchens of the Governor General who had his own special cooks.

The two slit-peepholes for slave-purchases. They peeped through these, did the master-selectors, in order to make their choices; knowing that, if they ventured among the "mass," they would be torn apart.

The outdoor platform overlooking the large general court, where the Governor General stood, and from which he could inspect the slaves each day.

Oh.

No one -- well, no <u>Black</u> -- experiences Elmina without exhaustion, ache, rage, and a drained and helpless Oh. Especially if that one has gone into the dungeon cell where so many wildly died, and pressed the new-time pampered body against those shrieking walls -- as I did, as Henry did.

The scarred Elmina walls scare.

Calling walls.

After Elmina, a taxi driver takes us to Government Rest House -- a restaurant and rest-room and small motel combined. We have a lunch of pepper-steak, delicious fried potatoes, peas and onions, onion soup, thick puddingy fruit cocktail, bread and butter and coffee. Later, we sit out on a small veranda, furnished with tables and chairs, enjoying the sunshine, looking at banana trees, coconut trees, large lizards, the "plane" birds, large self-possessed roosters, and a little group of Afrikans of various ages, merrily talking, under a garden umbrella.

After lunch, the taxi driver takes us to a little restaurant-tavern to which the bus for Accra will come. At two thirty. It is now about one o'clock. We sit inside, where I have a Coca-Cola, and H. has a beer. After thirty or forty minutes I get up and walk to the door, looking out on the scene of peaceful liveliness. Then I suggest to H., who is reading about Ghana, that we both go outside and sit on a bench there, among the Ghanaians. We do. We sit among the "plane"-birds, which look enormous when they land, the semi-naked tots, who are eating oranges, the stately, confident grandmothers tending their grandchildren; there's a serious-looking teen-aged girl with quite long and thick black hair, having it braided outside the "Beauty Saloon" by a girl her own age, her quietly-concerned, intent and equally serious friend. The many women in blouse-skirt costumes have matching scarves wound deftly about their heads. In general, the men are friendlier than the women, who are wary. Some of these men warmly nod, or smile.

Suddenly we are aware that it is time for the bus to arrive -- because those same young girls -- the "head girl" with a pleasingly plumpish figure in rusty red, and her sister or friend, in blue, and pink, and green -- whom we had seen on the "up" trip, are there to sell, again, their appetizing little cakes, fried pies (delicious-looking little half-circle fruit pies that my mother and Aunt Ella used to make). They stand there, right in front of us, carefully arranging their wares so they will show to best advantage -- piling the pies so high you are sure they are going to tumble -- but they do not! -- and chatting with an animated calmness among themselves, or to their quiet little brother (or friend!), about ten years old, who is carefully making a basket-weave circle, with long brightly-colored straw wires. It is a pretty and intricate little thing, and I ask if it is for sale. The three Business People look sardonically at each other, then burst into often-to-be-repeated giggles and Twi-chatter. (Is it Twi? It could be Ga. I know very little of any of the African languages.) I ask the price. More giggles. Then, "Sixty! Sixty pesetos." I tell the little brother to finish it, and of course I give him a full cedi, just as the Accra bus hauls in -- and before Young Brother had quite completed his bright-strawed work. Big Sister Head Girl is so surprised and, obviously, pleased by this unexpected windfall that, although she is indubitably a hard-boiled little businesswoman -- probably necessarily -- she, seeing me looking at her through a bus window, after I'm finally seated, smiles with open, merry, unwary kindness, waves at me, with old-friend brightness.

Back to Accra. Just as we arrive in the city, it starts to rain quite heavily. This is, after all, the rainy season and there are supposed to be thirteen rainy days in June.

A short rest, then dinner in the hotel dining room. For the first time, the meal is not good. "Mixed grill" -- doubtless retrieved from Sunday's leftovers; only the liver in the "mixed grill" is good.

I end the day mulling over the Significant Exchange with that young Cape Coast businesswoman, the hard-boiled one. Henry had said to her "We Blacks in the United States envy you. You ARE AFRIKANS. You KNOW this country is YOURS -- that you BELONG here. We Blacks in the United States don't know what we are." She had looked at him, with impatient semi-contempt. "YOU AmeriCAINE!"

For her, it was simple. For her, it was not to be questioned, not to be examined. She may or may not have known a thing about her Black brothers and sisters of yore, hauled against their will, long ago, to that strange country where, surely, everyone is rich and happy.

We spend one day visiting Kumasi, the Ashanti capital. Poet-publisher Dudley Randall's painter friend, Leroy Mitchell (Detroit) is teaching art at the University of Kumasi. He and his candid, sprightly wife Dorothy live in a large, airy, charmingly furnished house that speaks of

Africa and Detroit. Dorothy tells us that the women of Ghana are changing rapidly. They are not, in 1974, what they were in 1964. They are determined to secure further control over their money, their marriages, their minds. (The proper name for such a businesswoman as my Cape Coast friend is "Market Woman.")

Dorothy and Leroy take us on a little tour of Kumasi. We see the University, clean, good-looking; on its grounds, impressive student sculpture which Leroy has influenced. We are told the story of the Golden Stool. In 1900 an English attempt to sit upon it, to show the Ashantis Who's Boss, resulted in a bloody battle -- because the Golden Stool, the would-be conquerors were to understand, must be respected as a sacred cultural Symbol, keeper of the soul of the Ashanti nation.

On the highway, we see those famous trucks, carrying crops for the market, or passengers galore, called "mammy wagons" -- with those wonderful inscriptions on their sides, as: "The Lord Is My Shepherd -- I Don't Know Why"; "Friends Today -- Enemies Tomorrow"; "Paddle Your Own Canoe."

BLACK WOMAN IN RUSSIA

'We must tell each other as much as possible about each other.'

_Professor Alexander I. Ovcharenko, at the Soviet-American Writers' Conference, 1982.

I went into Russia armed with mental pictures of marching men, wide peasant women in shapeless skirts and long-sleeved flannel toppers tied with string. I expected to see dark babushkas galore. I expected to experience flavorless cabbage, greasy borscht; a grim landscape, grim babies, grim mothers and fathers. Russia. Land of the cold heart, the regimented mien.

It was the summer of 1982.

No, I didn't "read up" on the country before I went there. I wanted fresh impressions, fresh assaults on a chiefly unschooled consciousness.

I was invited by Harrison Salisbury (dead now) to attend the Sixth Annual Soviet-American Writer's Conference. The travelers included Charlotte Salisbury, Mr. and Mrs. Arthur Schlesinger, Jr., Mr. and Mrs. Irving Stone, Studs and Ida Terkel, Pepperdine University Chancellor Norvel Young and Mrs. Young, Pepperdine Dean and Mrs. Olaf Tegner, authors Robert Bly, Erica Jong, Susan Sontag.

Harrison Salisbury was, in addition to being the former assistant managing editor and associate editor of the *New York Times*, a specialist in Soviet affairs. He had traveled to many parts of the Soviet Union, and had written several books. I knew I was fortunate to have as a guide the author of *The Nine Hundred Days: The Siege of Leningrad.*.

We were to spend four days in the Ukraine, in clean Kiev, exchanging views with writers Nikolai Fedorenko, Grigol Abashidze, Chinghiz Aitmatov, Mikhail Alexeyev, Genrikh Borovik, Oles Gonchar, Mikhail Dudin, Pavlo Zagrebelny, Yasen Zasursky, Mstislav Kozmin, Vitaly Korotich. Then we were to spend several days in Leningrad, and several days in Moscow.

The American writers, coming from their several parts of the country, met July 20 at Kennedy Airport, Scandinavian Air Lines Lounge. We boarded a plane for Copenhagen. Ideal flight, proud pilots. When we reached Copenhagen, one of them announced "We can now tell you that there were three pilots in this cockpit and for this landing not a one of us touched the instruments. You have just had an absolutely perfect automatic landing!" We shivered, not with delight.

From my notes: "We check in at the Royal Hotel, after a *long* airport hike and a bus ride. I have a lovely *private* room, which is what I hoped for. All of us "singles" have private rooms. I'm to meet Studs and Ida Terkel for dinner, after I have a nap. In 1014, I have a two-hour nap, and I iron my clothes, and I take a bath. Fruit is sent in by the hotel management. With the Terkels, poet Robert Bly, and Vera Dunham (born in Russia, with much information to provide, about Russian literary personalities - who's "good," who's "bad," who "writes well," who *doesn't* "write well," etc.)— dinner at the Belle Terrace in the Tivoli, a Riverview-ish enclosure across the street from the Royal Hotel. After dinner we see a circus act outdoors: a family of red-covered acrobats, standing on each other or silently jumping off heads and high-flung chairs. I tell Robert Bly the story I have heard about his three-or-four hour readings, and how, at one of them, there being no door to use without disturbing the entire assemblage, the students began to leave, one by one and two by two, out of the back windows. Whether Robert is happy to have this bit of information or is *not* happy to have this bit of information I cannot tell. His face is stiff. Back to the hotel.

Flight SU-222 to Moscow, for an introductory Soviet blessing. We are met by smiling welcomers, given flowers and refreshments, and Russian money for "spending change." Chief among our guides is "Michael," Mikhail Kusmenko, twenty-one, who looks quite like the sensitive-faced actor Michael York, or as York looked in *Cabaret*. This Michael (Misha) is warmly solicitous, busily helpful to us all, *very* proud of his excellent English. Michael is everybody's favorite. He travels with us to Kiev, and smilingly helps escort us throughout our stay.

Each of the three hotels is beautiful, well-furnished, cheerfully serviced. Sovetskaya Hotel in Moscow, Kiev Hotel in Kiev, Hotel Europeiskaja in Leningrad.

In Kiev, the writers, Soviet and American, meet in a large yellow building, handsome, with great rooms, magnificent stair cases, shining floors, high ceilings. The rooms are rich with decoration and planting. Guards are anxious to help, to answer any questions. The atmosphere: a dignified but excitingly pregnant quiet.

In one particularly long, particularly noble room, are two "opposing" tables, for the two "opposing" representations, American and Soviet. (At one point during our proceedings, the second day I believe it was, Studs Terkel, briskly cheery, urged a shuffling: *Why should all Russians be sitting at a table together? - why should all the Americans be sitting at a table together? that* was the trouble in the world today! Let's mix it up a bit! - let's be really *together!* Nice little murmurings from the Russian side. Nice little murmurings from the American side. There is an immediate result, a rustle, an excited rustle; a charitable change. And for the duration of our get-together Studs Terkel is at the Soviet table with Russians. The rest of us remain in our appointed places.) There is simultaneous translation. Everyone feels comfortable enough to speak freely, and does. Arthur Schlesinger is drily analytical, drily critical.

Harrison Salisbury is universal. Erica Jong wants to know: "Where are the women writers? *Where* are the *women* writers?" She is informed, rather sheepishly, that they are all on vacation. "Out in the country." This is not the last time that Erica is to ask her irritating question. The Russian writers know (somehow) that Erica, (long-haired, shapely, and always beautifully dressed, having brought oodles of expensive clothes) has written sexy books, and I have the impression that they are prepared to make light of her. At first they trade rascally quips with her. They are surprised and discomfited when her major speech at the table turns out to be brilliant, informed, managed, sane.

Robert Bly and I are invited to read our poetry. Robert -- Fedorenko loves calling him that, with every letter in the name magically distinct -- accompanies himself on the mandolin (I think that is what it is) and in the high emotion of the moment leaps up and strides toward the center of the room, thus, of course, losing the labor of his translating equipment. "R-Ō-B-E-R-T!" shouts Fedorenko. "Don't get excited, R-Ō-B-E-R-T! Take i'*teasy*! Sit down! Take i'*teasy.* "

Among the poems I offer is my longish "The Life of Lincoln West." detailing the traumas of a little Black boy who, in a roundabout way, begins to recognize and value his identity. Fedorenko is enthralled. Missing my point entirely, he rhapsodizes over little Lincoln. He tells us all, and at length, about a dear little Black boy who had wandered into the midst of heretofore dense folk (including himself). This little boy everyone found _touchable_ and absolutely _darling_ "with his nice white teeth and nice rough hair. Everyone _loved_ to pat his nice rough hair." Afterward, away from the congratulatory tables, Russian and American, everybody is _pleased_ with me. I ponder on this, and I begin to get very angry. I get angrier and angrier. And I am sorrowful. Two meetings later I request attention. ("PLEASE call on me, Mr. Salisbury!"). And I read the following to the congregation:

"I agree with Mr. Aitmatov - a nuclear blast would abolish everything, _including_ all aspects of ethnic concern for ethnic bliss. Nevertheless, I am going to call attention to _Blackness_, a matter no one else here feels any _reason_ to cite." (I am, of course, the only Black in the room and often, it seems to me, the only Black in the whole of Russia, although that is nct true: sometimes I see a young Black male student in the street - and shortly before lunch on this very day I have seen a whole cluster of young African basketball players from, as I recall, Zaire, and run to semi-kiss them. During my three weeks away, entire, I am to see not one other Black woman, although I've been told by Russia-traveling friends that there is an "ample" contingent of Black women living in Russia. No Russian wants to talk about this, however. I'm looked at strangely, when I'm inclined to mention it, am abruptly left alone in the middle of the floor!) But to resume. To continue with my statement:

"No one *else* here feels any *reason* to cite Blackness because on the Soviet side there is very little association with Blacks. Soviets *see* very few. And on the *American* side there is as little association with Blacks as can comfortably be managed, although there is great opportunity in the United States of America, where there are many many many many many MANY Blacks. Well, all of you must understand that the planet is swarming with *dark* people. The other day Nikolai Fedorenko, droll, dry, and when he's right AND when he's wrong, a strangely fascinating personality, out of the kindness of his heart (and I received it as such) 'comforted me' with a tale of a *dear* little Black boy whom everyone found *touchable*, and absolutely darling with his nice white teeth . . . . . Then Mr. Fedorenko said something *very large*: "WE NEVER PAID ANY ATTENTION AT ALL TO THE FACT THAT HE WAS NEGRO."!!!!!!!!i WELL, I have to reply to this. *Essential* Blacks - by that I mean Blacks who are *not* trying desperately to be white - are happy to have you notice that they do not look like you. *Essential* Blacks don't *want* to look like you. *You're* OK, *they're* OK. We essential Blacks do *not* think it would be a blessing if everyone was of the same hue. Personally, I like the idea of a garden rich with varieties of flowers. Although I like roses, I like other flowers too. So please DO, Mr. Nikolai Fedorenko, go right ahead and *notice* that Blacks really look and *are* quite

different from yourself. Go right ahead and PAY
ATTENTION to that FACT!!!"

Well-covered middle-aged women clean the streets of
Kiev, paying an almost affectionate attention to their
work.

Seeing the Russian people in the street — watching
them adjust their little girls' BIG floppy bow-ribbons
which adorn the tops of the neatly groomed heads —
watching them adjust the behavior of frisky little boys —
watching them converse with each other, smiling,
clutching fondly their inevitable collections of two, three,
four or more flowers which, work-time over, they are
taking home — I decide that these swarms of human-faced
people do not <u>want</u> to be blown to bits. They want to go on
making those little dough pies with blueberry or cherry
sauce. They want to go on patting into position their
daughters' enormous bow-ribbons. They want to go on
taking flowers home.

Chekov had a warm involvement with the *details* of
Russian personality. It is easy to feel I am observing the
source of much Chekovian copy. Much Tolstoyan copy,
much Dostoievskian copy.

St. Cyril's Church, Kiev: plastered with religious
paintings. One of them in particular seizes me: a thin,

coal-black *devil*, with protruding teeth (you just know the artist considered this blackness the essence of evil "incarnate"!) seemingly scolding a plump, paunchy nude white man, sitting, doctor's-patient-wise, with a towel over his knees......

Before we leave clean Kiev for Leningrad (we are told that Kiev is irresistible in *all* seasons, but best in May, when the chestnut trees are in bloom), we go short distances to special features of Soviet history. Visits to a sixteenth-century poor man's cottage, and a nineteenth-century *rich* man's cottage. Equally rustic. Well, not quite. A boat ride down the Dnieper River to Kanev - pronounced *Kahn*-yev. The water of the Dnieper River is the cleanest, clearest river water I have ever seen. On the good-looking well-equipped boat we are fed generously: good dark bread with cheese, coffee, tea, salami, candy, fruit. In Kanev, we visit the memorial to the loved poet Taras Schevchenko, and the Schevchenko Museum.

I go with some of the others to a beautiful festival of folk songs and dances; such innocent joyfulness; we sit in the grass, before a stagefull of these colorfully costumed people - and are transported.

Babiy Yar. Near Kiev's city limits. Not until I go there do I understand, fully, what Yevgeny Yevtushenko did for us in writing that poem, long since a classic. What used to be a high-banked deep ravine, with a water bottom in which children once played, is now an arranged green with a look of deceitful peace. Because no one can be peaceful in this presence. Ninety thousand Jewish people, young and old, were herded here, beaten and shot to death by German soldiers, and buried here, in three days of September, 1941. The trees outside the bitter circle look vaguely indignant and reproachful.

In Russia I didn't see anybody who was scrawny or hunger-bellied. although the only *non-glorious* housing I was taken into was the hazardous apartment of the impulsive and rousing poet Bella Akhmadulina, who gave us an impromptu party. I certainly saw in the streets swarms of unedited Russian people. These looked, for the most part, healthy, energetic, well-fed. In the town streets are many, many galloping young women wearing smart little suits, ornate hair, stylish high heels . . . After a Writers' Union meeting, a grim Babiy Yar film — bulldozers rolling tons of the dead — little children and young girls and their elders of all ages stripping to be shot, burned or bitten. . . .

On July 29, departure for Leningrad, by Aeroflot. (Grim-looking plane, with seats close and uncomfortable.) Leningrad, "cradle of the Revolution". . . Sobering visit to cemetery containing thousands of Leningrad dead, German-killed; the steady mourning-music, insistent, pressuring, distressing. . . .On July 30 -- through the

Winter Palace to get to the Hermitage: The Rembrandts are proudly cited by our guide -- there are paintings, paintings! paintings galore; and there are treasures of jewelry, jewel boxes, jewel-encrusted swords, capes red and jewel-encrusted, gold rings, gold necklaces, gold bracelets, all richly wondrous . . .

St. Isaac's Cathedral: All these cathedrals we are to see are high-vaulted beauties sumptuously decorated, with impressive, large works of art throughout, and magnificent huge, engraved, intimidating inner doors . . . . . A drive through country scenes with non-lush grass (a frequent Russian sight) to Peter the Great's Summer Palace. . . .

Part of *my* visit's spectacle is our Company's Susan Sontag, whose statuesque dark Jewish beauty strides through Russia, always in slacks: always with one frontal white streak in the otherwise black hair: determinedly intellectual. She is not like Erica, who brought heavy suitcases of dresses, shoes, makeup. Susan at lunch: "Why are the *wives* here?" (meaning the American wives Mrs. Irving Stone, Mrs. Harrison Salisbury, Mrs. Arthur Schlesinger, all of whom are writers of distinction, and the wives of the dean and chancellor of Pepperdine University.) It was fascinating sitting behind Susan on the whizzing Intourist bus: "I have *two* books on him. . . .I have *four* books on him. . . .I have *four* translations on him. . . .I have *that* author in SIX translations". . . .Her

companion: "Oh! One of the most beautiful bridges!"
Susan: "Yes. I've seen *pictures* of it." Her companion:
"*That's a -*" Susan immediately: "Yes, I read about it long
before I came here."

. . . .Susan got very "mad" at me in Leningrad. Her
back had been listening, as we waited for a palace
admission, to Freda Lurye, an editor of *Foreign Literature*,
the highly respected Russian magazine, who was
questioning me, as she had been doing for days,
relentlessly: What Does It Mean To Be Black? Susan
begins to inform her. I <u>burn</u>. I address Freda. I say
(approximately) "Why do you turn from me to her with
this question? Obviously, being Black, I know more about
What It Means To Be Black than does *she.*" Susan
(approximately): " How *dare* you assume such Nonsense"
(her rage capitalizes the word) etc. etc. etc., in agitated
spew. By now we are entering this palace, and are
proceeding to the little anteroom where we must remove
our shoes, for the Russians are lovingly protective of
their palace floors. Susan is screaming. My outrageous
fancy that I know more about Being Black than *she* knows
has pushed her to wild-eyed frenzy. We are sitting beside
each other on the low wooden bench provided for shoe-
removing. She continues to scream. Finally, she utters an
unforgettable sentence - which I can report exactly,
because I wrote it down immediately: "I TURN MY BACK
UPON YOU." And she does. She carries out this awesome

threat. She turns her Back upon me, with a gr-r-eat shake of her bottom to appall me.

I am ass—uredly impressed.

Of course, S.S. had every right to resent my jumping into her Possession of a conversation. I was guilty of a breach of etiquette. So were the hosts of the Boston Tea Party.

At a concert, with merry singing and variety acts, and dainty little dances, it occurred to me that there is a certain Innocence about the Russian people. It's a puzzle. Or at least it is puzzling to *us*, the American "sophisticates," so used to dirt, disarray, degradation. Young Russian people (great cigarette-smokers, incidentally) claim to know nothing of drugs or drug-running. They claim to know nothing of really *violent* crime. Their stage-shows may have advanced to increased flesh-revelation, but the meticulous little dancers never *really* let themselves go. I haven't seen EVERYBODY, of course, but I would venture to say there are no Tina Turners over here. No Richard Pryors. No Eddie Murphys. No porno shows. . . .(?)

The Leningrad Writers' Union: At each of our arrivals we have been *met* with flowers and handshakes from smiling Writers' Union people. Here in Leningrad at the Writers' Union special meeting we are afforded buttered bread with caviar, coffee, vodka, and other amenities. Erica Jong stands up and mourns the absence of "the women writers." (Again.) We are told by a jesting director, stout and businessman-looking, that the men have sent their writing wives off to summer resort, it being summer, yok-yok. But before Erica J.'s assault, Harrison Salisbury has called on me to lead the self-"explanations." I say to this Leningrad contingent, "My name is Gwendolyn Brooks. I'm a Black poet - you can see that. And I want to say how much I appreciate this opportunity to meet Russian people, and how much I appreciate their welcoming kindness." Later, I read my poem for Michael, to wild applause (these people, these Russian people, are warmly serious about poetry, they *feel* and love poetry). The poem is translated, a bit, by cold-voiced, imperious Marina, one of our Leningrad guides, then it is taken over by Sasha (Alexander), who claims the right "because-I-have-seen-this-poem." A major announcement. "I *know* this poem." Michael - Mikhail Kusmenko - ("Mischa") is merrily disgruntled by the translation, saying to me, "My eyes now are not 'quick' and 'smart', but 'beautiful'!!!!! I say "That's OK, Michael, they are beautiful too!!!!" I'm having fun with nice little Sasha's twist of my language - but Michael says with serious shyness, "Thank you."

. . . .Dostoievsky. The Apartment. His last apartment. Round-top black hat in the little entrance hall (his hat). Umbrellas (not his but typical of the time.)

Clusters of family pictures on the papered walls. Dining room - no carpet now nor formerly the guide assures us - with handsome heavy furniture; on the dark table a samovar, large, heavily flourishing, ready for tea; a buffet with comely dishes and cups. The Study! - where D. wrote. The ponderous, wide, red-pattern upholstered sofa, on which he died, and which is right behind the heavy, large desk, on which we see his last half glass of tea - supposedly!! "I won't drink the tea," promises Irving Stone (now dead) when he requests permission to sit in D's chair and to hold D's pen. ("Now that you've let me hold the pen, may I hold it again, and have my wife take a picture" - which is done, to the music of incredulous gasps by myself and the Terkels.) We see the nursery, with a map on the wall, a doll, picture books, a rocking horse. Then we are taken by Ganna, the delightful, giggly, prettily plump, dark-haired little curator of this Dostoievsky Museum, to the narrow room that, she tells us, once served as a kitchen -- two large Dostoievsky family portraits have been introduced to a wall. Here, at a round table, Ganna, her quietly efficient assistant helping her, serves us tea, delicious tea, with Lorna Doone-ish cookies; and those little chocolate candies twisted in colorful manipulations of that waxy paper you have encountered before in Russia. Minor biographical details from Ganna Bograd, who gives us, also, a little book she has written about D., and descriptive materials partly in English. How pleasant! Possibly the most purely pleasant and charming half hour I am to spend in Russia. Downstairs we find the

Terkels (the Terkels had gone downstairs before tea, Studs pleading weariness). Studs is enjoying mightily what we hear, in our clearer state, a semi-drunkenly offered piece. The singer is a very flirtatious "Anatoly."

August 2, 1982 - Last day in Leningrad; we go to one last palace, with glittery, much-decorated rooms. Here, Harrison Salisbury speaks in affectionate Russian to a tiny woman serving as a door attendant. She lights up when she hears this American using her own beloved language. He asks if she has lost someone in the siege of Leningrad. She has. She is reluctant to say goodbye to him. . . .Pushkin's school. I see his first school-written lines . . . .The Salisburys and I visit the neat, light apartment of Alexandr Blok. . . . Nice train to Moscow at 11:55 p.m., arriving in Moscow at 8:30 a.m. (after a tasty breakfast with hot tea, served us in our attractive compartments.) It's the Sovetskaya Hotel. . . .We visit one of Tolstoy's houses, a mighty house in the country. In a large case, his bicycle, two pairs of boots he made for friends. His office holds a big desk, a sofa, quite like the imposing sofa on which Dostoievsky died. To the right of the desk, against the wall, is a large writing or drawing stand. In this office Tolstoy wrote one hundred works. Quite dark, this office. . .

. . .Old old women within the protecting walls of cathedrals. Some with winter coats (on August fourth). . .

No matter how shabby or decrepit a house, presence of the customary flowers or flower! gracing windows. On the streets, always, both men and women, carrying flowers home. Just a few, wrapped in skimpy paper, or not wrapped. . . .The woods are quiet and beautiful and reaching - and there are many: but in Moscow, I observe, *almost* all green areas are weedy. Sometimes you see old women in babushkas, wide dresses, and worn heavy shoes, weeding the green. Some of these weeders' dresses are thinned-out cotton, over which there may be worn sad blue or green or dust-pink sweaters, listlessly buttoned over wide square bodies or *other* bodies with billowing bellies. . . .Afternoons: plump women sitting, not on their porches, but in front of their fences. . . .These substantial women may be seen, also, in bus-stalls, at bus-lines, stalls provided with benches painted over with red and yellow, or stripes. . . . .Interiors: many interiors, seen from the street -- just a sneak's-eye view -- reveal themselves as drear, drab, sad . . . .Wet clothes hang here, as in the States. . . .hang from windows - from clotheslines - over lines of fence. Familiar itemata: I am repeatedly impressed by the numbers of old women. . . .here is a woman praying, behind a locked cathedral door, making her Catholic signs. Then she strides her short, enhanced self down the rocky road. . .Father Paul, at the Zagorsk seminary, and the Zagorsk cathedral. . . . Then another cathedral where, when people, any people, any private people, are moved to commemorate a family member or loved friend, they come in groups to sing in beautiful rich Russian voices...Question: How are the songs chosen? — for the choices should suit everyone.

Moscow. We're snug in the Sovetskaya. Elegant staircases, sedate halls, fine furnishings, fine dining room, fine food. (Throughout this Russian trip we've had delicious food. Non-slimy borscht! Rich dark bread. Tomatoes and cucumbers galore. Shishkebab, fruits, ice cream. And, outdoors, excellent ice cream cones, much loved by the populace. Apple tarts. Veal, lamb, beef, pork, chicken, fish. Guava preserves. Potatoes in various arrangements. Heavy soups. The popular little dough pies also, but I refuse to eat dough.)

The trip to Zagorsk, for more tours through more museums and distinguished churches, with their leaders in conscious regalia. . . .A visit to the Kremlin - but we are treated to very little of it, and that little we are whisked through rapidly. Such a whirlwind exterior tour leaves me with no clear impression. On the fast trip to Zagorsk, I see - with difficulty - open doorways that afford views of gloomy, ragged, desperate interiors. Guide Marina does not want to answer any questions about these. She is, in fact, getting quite sick of my days-long questions about "houses." "May we see some of the houses?" Answers are vague or vacuous. Eventually, in reference to an isolated non-grand but non-horrible square, Marina barks angrily, "*There's* a house, Gwen-do-lyn. You wanted to see *houses.* "

In the packed downtown streets of Moscow, the Russian people seem to be walking all in a single parade, a compact parade. The tempo is similar, at least on the neat top, to that of United States downtowners.

Before we leave Moscow we are guests at Ambassador Hartman's mansion. Sumptuous. An open, modern, sophisticated splendor. The ambassador's wife greets me warmly, because she has known and, she says, loved my poetry for many years. Bella Akhmadulina is there. As you read her poetry you feel that you've got a nervous little worm in 'possession' - a bright, twisty, unexpectedly wise little worm; and meeting her personally, you feel exactly that! It is on this occasion that Bella carts some of us off, post-reception, to the rinky-dink apartment she shares with her present husband, who paints, sculpts, creates set designs. Bella was once married to Yevtushenko. You reach the wild, pouty apartment via a tiny, rickety elevator, which can take only five of us at a rising. We rise by fives, and are returned by fives to the vast cold spirit of the first floor. Escape.

What else is Moscow to me? What further "knowledges" of Moscow do I gather to bring home? The beautiful information that it is safe to walk anywhere in Moscow, day or night. The appealing fact that so very many of the citizenry go home from work carrying flowers - a bunch of them, or a few. It is not true that Russians are "rude." I encountered curiosity here and there, that translated into puzzlement that a Black woman was walking their streets, but chiefly I encountered pleasantness, smiling or unsmiling "tolerance," or downright cheery welcoming. An author's wife, after our forty minutes or so of casual conversation, hugged me fiercely, exclaiming loudly "We _like_ you!". . . .Such a serious appreciation of poetry. One poet asks me the size of a customary edition of poetry in the United States. I reply that, if a poet in the United States sells an edition of five thousand copies, he or she is "doing well." My questioner is amazed, and declares that in Russia an edition of a _hundred_ thousand copies is perfectly ordinary. Listening, I remember that Yevtushenko and Voznesensky have recited, often, to audiences of fourteen thousand or more. And I remember what celebration enveloped me because I wrote a poem about Michael!. . . .It is not true that Moscow audiences sit dull-eyed through theater or opera performances. I see the same smiles and shining eyes, hear the same gasps, giggles and happy frequent applause as I find in Chicago, New York, San Francisco and Peoria. . . .Here plump stomachs are OK! I see hundreds and hundreds of them! - male and female stomachs out-thrust and non-apologetic! - I _do_ glimpse _some_ cozy little houses, behind fences. . . .I love seeing the babies in the strollers, pushed by young mothers in neat red sweaters, blue sweaters, print dresses. . . .It is _not_ true that all Russians feel pounded. . . .It _is_ true that the loved children are spectacularly well-behaved. . . .Good-looking modern clothes are the norm, not the exception. . . .I meet Moscow people who explain Soviet uneasiness by pointing to a symbol such as the siege of Leningrad - a million and a half deaths in nine hundred days. In short, "all we" are watchful because when we have not been watchful we have been assailed, and assailed, and assailed. . . (Forgot to record that, in a Leningrad park, we saw a famous statue of the highly respected Black poet Alexander Pushkin. Susan Sontag got as close as she could, spread her arms wide and shrieked "My Pushkin! My Pushkin!" I wish I had a picture of that.)

Another of my knowledges: Certainly those who have not visited this part of the world are ineligible to vote on what it is or is not.

When I disembark at Copenhagen's airport I observe instantly that what Jean Stone, Irving's wife, had said to me is true: "You'll notice brightness. You notice a difference *immediately*, sharply!" I do, I do. First of all, there is an unmistakable, feelable presence of hope in the air, noticeable on this second "experience" of Copenhagen as, logically, it had not been on the first. This is not to counter-suggest that the Russians looked miserable, but hope was not what I saw as their aura; what I saw as their aura was sanction.

In the Copenhagen airport: abundance. Abundant
wares. Cheeses and sausages and candies and games and
jewelry and clothing.

In New York: cough drops. And lots and lots of
beautiful Blackness all around me.

I want to close with that poem I wrote for Michael. It
says what I think of the essential spirit of youth in Russia.

MICHAEL, YOUNG RUSSIA

To Mikhail Kusmenko, twenty-one years old.
From a Black Woman
born in America — whose origin is Afrika.

Michael, I see you!
In the Russian winter.
The lights in your quick, smart eyes
are dancing with snow-sparkle.
You ski; you skate over the ice.
In your heart you shout
"I *breathe*! I am *alive*!
My body is moving!
My body knows life is good and my body responds!
I am a straight response, a Reverence!
And I love all the people in the world!"

Michael --

I see you in the woods of Moscow and Kiev,
affectionate with deer and branch and flower.

Young Russia!
You are an affectionate spirit,
with arms stretched out to
life and love and truth and Celebration,
with arms stretched out to
what is clean and kind.

Thursday, July 29,1982, Kiev

(With sincere respect and admiration for one of the finest
young men I ever met.)

From Michael, Christmas, 1982 — a beautiful card
showing St. Basil's with Santa Claus in a sleigh before it:

Dear Gwendolyn:

I hope very much that you haven't forgotten me. I
want to wish you and yours the best of everything for
1983. I treasure evergreen memories of our meeting and
your poem. I'll be happy to meet you again some day.
Meanwhile, my warmest regards and friendly love.

Always, Misha.

THE DAY OF THE GWENDOLYN

The Library of Congress
May 5, 1986

My daughter was proud of me on the thirtieth of September, when I gave my first Consultant's reading in Coolidge Auditorium. I can see her still, shining-eyed in the first row, jumping up and applauding me. And I remember her post-enthusiasm: "Oh Mama! -- it was The Day Of The Gwendolyn."

From The Library of Congress Information Bureau, February 16, 1987:

"Gwendolyn Brooks Summarizes Her Year As the 29th Consultant in Poetry."

Each year Library divisions and departments prepare annual reports of their activities. The Library's Consultants in Poetry are not spared this obligation, and the annual report of the Consultant is a segment of the Manuscript Division's report. Gwendolyn Brooks' report is so distinctive that it is printed below. It formed part of her final lecture presentation as Consultant, May 5, 1986.

So many times since last May, when I was invited to be the 29th Consultant in Poetry to the Library of Congress - I have been asked *What* does the Consultant in Poetry *do?* The question is accompanied by a smile. The general understanding is that the Consultant in Poetry does *nothing.* Of course, many people *laugh* when they hear the word "poet." Being a poet, it is supposed, is akin to being a lunatic.

Knowing this to be such a popular conclusion, I have been impressed by the respect and concern afforded the Consultant's office by everyone here connected with it. Daniel Boorstin, John Broderick, Nancy Galbraith, Jenny Rutland, John Sullivan, efficient and pleasant Emma Vaughan — all have treated my work, my ideas, my preferences with respect, concern and warm enthusiasm. Semi-saint John Broderick, assistant librarian for research services, has labored mightily and graciously to get the people here whom I wanted to introduce to you. Cheery, expert, cooperative, friendly, self-effacing John "Communications" Sullivan! Poetry associate Nancy Galbraith — not only brilliant and knowledgeable in an assortment of areas, but the magnificent wheel-oiler Upstairs. Because of her mysteriously expert influence, achievements <u>seem</u> seamless. She has coordinated my matters — appointments, rearrangements, visitor reception, general clarification — with what seems to me a special genius. Jenny Rutland — our second poetry associate - new-penny bright, reliable, hard-working, genial and generous.

And I salute the Washington, D.C., Maryland, and Virginia Community. I have been amazed by my reception. Here in the Library I'm greeted with kindly respect and sincere smiles not only by research people, directors, professors and other staff, but also by officers, Security, elevator operators, gift shop clerk, Mr. Cronin, House Page English teacher, all of the House and Senate pages, for whom I've read and whom I feel like hugging whenever I see them, so sunny-faced, intelligent and <u>rollicking</u>. Dr. Jerry Ainsfield, my sunny next-door professor-neighbor. Maids and handymen, too.

Well, I have never worked so hard in my life! I have never been so exhausted, but gloriously exhausted, at the end of a day, *Or*, at the end of a night, since *some* days have been 9 a.m. to 11:30 p.m. "days." If you're puzzled! - some Mondays and Tuesdays I've stayed in my office on the Third Floor until time for a Coolidge Auditorium poet-presentation, meanwhile answering letters, planning my little programs, sorting files, etc. After that 8 p.m. reading or lecture there is, as you know, a reception, from which Nancy and Jenny and I, Security and the servers are the last to leave. I mentioned Mondays and Tuesdays: those are the working days I was *allowed to choose.* I threw in Wednesdays, 9 a.m. to 3:30 p.m., because otherwise I could not have handled the enormous mail that had to be answered, nor the many, many visitors, local and for eign, I was pleased to receive. (There have been exceptions, of course: on certain pre-arranged dates I have been out of the office because of campus-visiting in other states.)

Among foreign visitors to my office, sometimes accompanied by excellent interpreters, were writers and critics from Poland, Czechoslovakia, Peru, Jordan, Turkey, Malawi, Pakistan, Mexico, Uruguay, Argentina, Costa Rica, Bolivia, El Salvador, Colombia. These people came to the Poetry Room, where we chatted and questioned, laughed, recited, exchanged narrative glances. When we parted, there was a strange, special warmth to share. Tears, too.

I found that a Consultant is left pretty much alone - encouraged to develop a personal direction. You enter with a reading of your poetry. You close with a lecture. Between those involvements you assist in the recording of poets (which I did not do: but I have left a list of estimable people who *should* be recorded here. See list appended). A Consultant recommends poets to read in the Coolidge Auditorium series of programs. A Consultant introduces the impressive writers who come here to speak, the Consultant's invitees and others. I can't tell you how much I have enjoyed that. I've had the privilege of introducing, among others, such significant creators as Doris Grumbach, William Golding, Keri Hulme, Les Murray,

Yevgeny Yevtushenko, Haki, Sonia Sanchez, Grace Schulman, Barbara Guest, Joyce Carol Oates, Michael Harper, Galway Kinnell, David Ignatow, Mari Evans, Mark Perlberg, Michael Anania, Sandra Cisneros, Garrison Keillor, Louis Simpson; and James Baldwin, who closed my season.

I have been interviewed, taped, and televised galore. At WETA I made the delightful discovery that Henry Taylor, new Pulitzer winner (poetry), was a student of mine at Indiana University 20 years ago. He met me at the door with a framed certificate signed by me and denoting that I had given him a $25 prize, which meant that I had chosen him as the best poet in my class. Time has taught me to be impatient with that word "best," of course. But Henry Taylor is a truly important poet. Familiar *and* strange.

I have visited innumerable schools - elementary schools, high schools, sometimes two or three in a day. I have visited area institutions such as Georgetown University, the University of Virginia, SUNY in Albany, the Community College of Baltimore, the Enoch Pratt Free Library of Baltimore. This spring, I have been crowned with four honorary doctorate degrees: from George Washington University, the University of Vermont, Spelman College in Atlanta, and Seattle University (for the last three I furnished commencement addresses). This little recital is appropos of nothing. I couldn't resist boasting.

I have visited the Maryland Correctional Facility in Jessup, reading, and enlisting the inmates in poetry-reading, giving them books of poetry, and joining in free discussion. I have visited, similarly, Lorton Prison. I have spoken to "the family," as it is called and regarded, at the Comprehensive Alcohol and Drug and Abuse Center, and was warmly received. I have spoken to and exercised with the Washington Seniors at their Wellness Center. I created my Lunchtime Reading Series, an intense success! From noon to presumably two p.m. in the Poetry Room, poets read, received, and enjoyed comment on their works, will, and temperament. Then I took them, with 20 or so audience members to lunch (I paid) at Toscanini or Monocle, where the delicious inquisition continued. I managed three of these Lunchtime Readings. The first featured Michael Weaver and Grace Cavalieri. The second featured six poets - Samuel Allen, Dolores Kendrick, Hannah Kahn, Meredith Skeath, Mani Philip, and Iona Harris. The third featured fourteen poets, opening with Washington's nine-year old Marcus Shaw and 17-year old Lucy Venable of South Carolina. The other 12 were: Margaret Walker, Ethelbert Miller, May Miller, Julia Fields, Ed Cox, Houston Baker, Toi Derricotte, Angela Peckenpaugh, Meredith Skeath, Josephine Jacobsen (a former Consultant), Kenneth McClane, Jane Lunin Perel. On April 23, Shakespeare's birthday, I had a Mini-Festival, with 29 poets reading - locals _and_ poets who had come from many parts of the country, honorariumless and paying their own expenses absolutely. (See Mini-Festival list appended.)

I have managed to excite many area youngsters _toward_ a realization that poetry can be nourishing and enhancing and, again, _extending._ I have not told these youngsters that handling paper and pencil will guarantee a Pulitzer prize. I tell them, chiefly, that poetry, written or read, can enrich and strengthen their lives. I tell that to other sizes of people too.

I have been stirred by the excitement evinced by Washington poets. It is contagious.

Those who are concerned about the words "Poet Laureate" being added to the title of Consultant need not be. The Administration of the Library of Congress in the past has shown great intelligence in selecting sane, talented, and discriminating people for this post - after all, it selected me, didn't it? - and will continue to do so. There is nothing to fear. And certainly Robert Penn Warren is an excellent poet, with many distinctions. It should be remembered, too, that next year there will be another Poet Laureate. And the next year there will be _another_ Poet Laureate. And the next year there will be _another_ Poet Laureate. And the . . . .

Poets to be recorded: A.R. Ammons, Margaret Atwood, Sandra Cisneros, Lucille Clifton, Edwin Honig, Ethelbert Miller, Lisel Mueller, Linda Pastan, Mark Perlberg, Sterling Plumpp, Michael Anania, Luis Omar Salinas, Meredith Skeath, Michael Weaver, Haki Madhubuti, Mari Evans.

Mini-Festival (One-Day) April 23, 1986 - Poetry Room. Poets read in the following order: Carlos Schaffenburg, Michael S. Harper, John Landry, Carolyn Kreiter-Kurylo, Grace Cavalieri, Stephen C. Wright, Eleanor Traylor, Lenard D. Moore, Betty Parry, Roberta Keller, Mani Philip, Garry Hutchinson, Nancy Galbraith, Jeanette Adams, Meredith Skeath, Mauri Saalakhan, Julia Fields, Daryl Stover, Hope Price, Clarence Thomas, Carol Gregory, Anthony Howard, Lamont Steptoe, Shaun Henderson, Myrtle Taylor, "Yvonne", Otis Williams, Misty Brown, Madalin Price.

--Gwendolyn Brooks
Library of Congress
Consultant in Poetry;
1985 — 1986

INTRODUCTIONS TO SPEAKERS AT THE LIBRARY OF CONGRESS, 1985-1986.
COOLIDGE AUDITORIUM

I was appointed as "Consultant in Poetry to the Library of Congress" in 1985 by Librarian Daniel Boorstin. Assistant Librarian John Broderick was my supervisor.

"You <u>demystified</u> the Library!" said Sonia Sanchez. She added that people of "all" kinds, intimidated by the Library's huge cool magnificence, had felt free to come past marble and gold to see me. True! To my great delight they came -- to talk about poetry. Male, female; from nine to ninety. Heterosexual, homosexual, etc. Jew. Gentile. Muslim. Aristocrat, beggar. Domestic, foreign. Senator, scientist. The sinful and the saintly. A bag lady.

The numerous underlinings in these little prefaces were <u>speaking</u> instructions to myself. I enjoyed writing these prefaces, enjoyed delivering them. Didn't have to be Brilliant. Didn't have to be Deep. Just had to prepare the audience to receive, with comfortable curiosity, or with sweet-sour excitement, what was to come: and to do this in Just A Few Minutes. <u>Very</u> important point. No audience -- no author waiting on the stage behind you -- wants to sit through an intro as long as the feature of the evening.

I imposed length on the Coolidge audiences only when absolutely necessary. For example: there were facts relative to Haki and Mari and Sonia and Garrison Keillor that I could rely on three and a half people to know.

FOUR CHICANO POETS

SANDRA CISNEROS, LUIS OMAR SALINAS, ALBERTO RIOS LORNA DEE CERVANTES

I am so glad that you came out tonight. If only because your children may be studying a plump Laurence Perrine anthology -- very popular in contemporary schools -- that carries not one poem by an Hispanic in <u>any</u> category.

I am proud to bring this poetry to your attention because numbers of <u>you</u> may not have met it. And if <u>that</u> is the truth, you have missed mystery. You have missed mastery. You have missed a poetry impudently varied, a poetry SINFULLY INVOLVED. (You <u>know</u> that today involvement is SIN.)

This poetry — these poetries — glitter, stalk, tiptoe or stomp, work with iron or silk or a combination of those. These POETRIES settle, sail out, or up-toss their inexorable jewels for <u>you</u> to catch and carry.

I'm not going to impose a mile-long introduction. (You're all going to sigh in relief!) We have four important people here. I hope each will define SELF.

We lend you -- alphabetically -- Lorna Dee Cervantes, Sandra Cisneros, Alberto Rios, Luis Omar Salinas.

MICHAEL ANANIA

Michael Anania's voice seems controlled. However, passion has formed it. As you read him or listen to him, you feel you are in the company of one who knows himself and you. He guides you through his landscape, recommending certifiables and improbables to your attention. Are you influenced? That is not his obsession. His obsession is his landscape; he seems to have a good deal of faith in your intelligence, and does not provide you with crutches or binoculars.

You may or may not interpret his demonstrations as <u>he</u> interprets them. In either case, he will be the first to say "Bravo." With a <u>continued</u> reliance on the shapeliness and strength of his own response.

DONALD HALL

Donald Hall leaves you asking questions about matters you thought you'd resolved, matters you thought you'd squared away.

And beneath the <u>technical</u> care, the scrupulous involvement with precision and balance, there is this fine joy.

Somehow, when you come out of a visit in Donald Hall's poetry, you have the idea that, in spite of what Dan Rather told him last night, he is pleased to get up in the morning.

He believes that "poems are made of words used efficiently." He believes good poetry "is the perfect machine of language."

He is an <u>open</u> theorist: he likes today's artist to allow <u>nothing</u> to escape consideration, he likes today's artist to act "as if restlessness were a conviction." He likes today's artist to tell self: "Keep <u>moving</u>."

Donald Hall is on <u>my</u> Short List of poets who, respecting poetry cleanly and honestly and reverently, do not pose at parties, smooth, cigaretted and tweed-casual, coldly analyzing and prescribing for poetry -- for ALL the arts in their "illness." He seems to believe that there's lots of Bounce, and that there will be a healthy survival.

A nice story I've just been told is that when he was a boy of sixteen he begged his mother to give him my first book for a Christmas present.

In the late Sixties, when the fires fell, and whites in the arts and everywhere else were being assailed devoutly and deliciously, Donald Hall was not intimidated. He felt vitality in the "Vile." Even the columns of obscenities in Kill-the-Honky poems delighted him, because he seemed to know, as few other white poets seemed to know, that the Eruption, the Perpetration, was a necessary statement -- a step in the development not only of a Poetry but of a People. He was an early champion of the "New Black Poetry." It took a lot of spunk in those years (and spunk is not a rampant commodity) to face your disapproving fellow-whites and announce: "This is authentic poetry. This is something rich and strange." Also, as a campus recommender, he employed many Black creators. (Not all white "pioneers" were on the Civil Rights lines.)

ETHERIDGE KNIGHT

Etheridge Knight is perceptive. His vision is merciless. He spares himself nothing, he spares you nothing.

Etheridge Knight is a Broadside Press poet. Many Broadside Press poets, through the language-testing dozen of years after 1966, were busy with maneuver and jolt, and the result was that, again and again, the astonished reader would be aware of an individual voice, would think "This poet sounds -- essentially -- like NO ONE ELSE."

You would say that to yourself even though early on you had understood that the general tools involved were the hot hand, the hot heart, HARD health.

Etheridge, I wish I could order your entire program. Don't let us lack "Hardrock" -- don't let us lack the heart-catching odd beauty, the nourishing heart-break of "The Idea of Ancestry"! "The Violent Space," and "As You Leave Me." The interior rhyming of "A Wasp Woman Visits A Black Junkie In Jail" ("Common, summon, human"!) The ruddy realism of "It Was A Funky Deal".....

Long ago I wrote a little poem called "Truth", identifying Truth as sunshine; the opening two lines were:

> "And if sun comes,
> how shall we greet him" _____

Later, Etheridge replied with superb irony

> "The sun came, Miss Brooks". . . .

Many, many visions visited your cell, Etheridge Knight -- and they educated you, they vaulted you.

Come here and open your mouth.

ANGELA JACKSON

Angela Jackson is an experimenter. She respects many people -- but she long ago decided not to sound like them. So she ended up sounding like Angela Jackson.

So many little twists and turns in her work! Rarely are you prepared for them. So many satisfying perceptions of actuals we recognize, remember, or are <u>now</u> ready to <u>learn</u>! Such impudent portraits of people -- people she paints or invents! Such combos of colloquial and obscure! -- <u>bound</u> to confound and delight!

Well, here is something <u>different</u> for your dinner!

Angela Jackson.

DORIS GRUMBACH

First of all, what you say about Doris Grumbach — if you are suitably attuned — if you are <u>ready</u> — is that she is absolutely comfortable with words and conditions. She has no fear (well, if she has WE don't see it!) — we feel that she is not uneasy nor self-doubting, that she does not stride-'n'-hide. Two other authors I've honored with such trust are British essayist Lytton Strachey and Black American poet Jean Toomer. Do you know what I mean by "trust" in this reference? I mean that, with Lytton and Jean and Doris, I feel that I can LEAN IN — that I will not be allowed to fall — that my Supports are reliable because they know so well their own milieu, their own tools and weapons, their own Whirling Space.

With a deft pen Doris Grumbach makes — for us — some human beings complete with shock and nuance — some people dirty clean mean and soft and stiff and strange and familiar and shadowy and sharp and shrieking and hushed and cold and hot and wise and stupid and amazingly cruel and superseding. Those are the qualities of the Grumbach populace: (and I feel I've left out a couple of conditions, conditions with which this author is concerned.)

Once introduced to the work of Doris Grumbach you want to find more of her books.

Doris Grumbach.

WILLIAM GOLDING

Returning to "Lord of the Flies", after many years, and finding Jack still there, "on top of the sow", still "stabbing downward with his knife" --- and realizing that it is, was and will be CERTAINLY the truth, and that, surely almost as horrible is the fact that we are, have been, and will be steadily stabbing ourselves and the other little pigs -- I am, for a proverbial moment, disoriented.

I rally, however. Because when you're my age you have long since made Survival Decisions, have told yourself that, no matter how sick and subterranean a lot of your friends think folks are and have to be, you will continue to respect such tenets as you have found serviceable and sustaining.

William Golding is a star and a stimulus to itch under because he delivers us to our messes and makes us assess our messes.

It is a pride to introduce you to the man who numbers first among his hobbies "THINKING" -- the exhilaratingly complex William Golding.

HAKI MADHUBUTI
SONIA SANCHEZ

The introducing is longer tonight, because I've a double introduction and one that seeks to put some things in place.

Both these poets, at times, have been called "racists". I define racism as Prejudice <u>With</u> Oppression. That is: you are permitted to detest green eyes. That's all right. That's personal. You are not permitted to kill every green-eyed individual you encounter. That's not all right. That's Oppression.

These two people are not killers. They are lovers of humanity, of what is human. They are interpreters and protectors of Blackness. They are subscribers to what is beautiful in the world.

They will offer you "<u>representative</u>" Black poetry.

My saying <u>that</u> does not assault our mutual understanding that there are respectable Black uniquities. However -- today many Black poets are flopping off in worrisome directions. Many of them do not know <u>what</u> to do or be. Many of them want above all things <u>not</u> to be Black. Black people who want above all things <u>not</u> to be Black are the most pitiable <u>and</u> comical people in the world. The poets among such <u>fight</u> Blackness with every

94

punch and pout in their power. Such people are very busy imitating the new moderns -- those manufacturers of chopped-up journalism, dazed and dopey. Such people have been fondled and adopted by non-spunky white poets and critics who of course have no interest in preserving, in enfirming the bolts, the binders, of Blackness. They would like Blackness to disappear altogether. In "defining" our work, they twist it to accommodate their needs.

INSERT: Oh dear. I know history may repeat itself. Do you know that precious last-Election story about Jesse Jackson? He was crossing a large body of water in a small boat -- with the Pope. It was windy. Suddenly, the Pope's little cap flew off his head. Then Jesse Jackson stepped out of the boat, walked across the water, retrieved the cap, walked back, clapped the cap on the Pope's head. Next morning, the newspaper streamers proclaimed: "JESSE JACKSON CAN'T SWIM!" _____ Well, ultimately (in all my non-grandeur), I may see captions announcing: 'GWEN BROOKS CALLS ALL WHITE CRITICS NON-SPUNKY!"

However.

Sonia Sanchez is an explorer. I have always thought of her as one of that quintet of Black people -- herself, Mari Evans, Don L. Lee (who became Haki), Etheridge

Knight, and Nikki Giovanni – all of whom admired the impudent spirit of Baraka, and who began, in '66 and '67, to turn Black poetry "around". I do not mean that these people suddenly spurted up in those years. They were all writing voluminously when I met them, and they were publishing too. Dudley Randall, poet and founder of Broadside Press, courageously published, platformed them all.

In the late sixties, the quintet and their Cohorts tried to do something fresh, defining Black poetry as poetry written "by Blacks, about Blacks, to Blacks." That word "to" has been wickedly translated, often, into "for." Any poetry is FOR any readers or listeners willing to investigate it. I believe all factions should be willing to investigate Black poetry. Black people -- I think -- will be around forever. Anyone is likely to meet them suddenly -- border, boardroom, boulevard, bistro, back alley, bathroom, bar. And it behooveth the Anyone to know what makes the breed tick.

Sonia and Haki have remained loyal to their early re-created essence. They like the word CONSISTENT.

Sonia can be mischievous. She called me up a while ago and said "Gwen, I want your permission to use the form you used in 'The Anniad' in "Annie Allen". I told her: "In no way does Sonia Sanchez need my permission to do anything she wants to do, but Sonia, that is not 'MY'

form: It's EUROPEAN." Even if she hadn't giggled, I
would have known Sonia was kidding. Of all our poets,
these two are LEAST likely to flop back into the Forties.
The language of Sonia Sanchez is her own best
introduction, of course. One of her serious and inclusive
avowals is this: "If you're going to say something, your
house must be in order, because there is so much disorder
outside." You will experience, in her product, lyricism
and steel. You will be aware of Sonia Sanchez as
committed poet, energized woman, necessary Black.

About Haki, pioneer. Haki respects Sonia, and she
respects him, as artist and as Family. Those who love and
those who loathe Haki agree that more than any other
Black poet who became influential in the late Sixties he
has remained actively loyal to the richness of his faith in
and love for Black people. He spanks them now and then,
but only as a benevolent father would spank them --
aching in his awareness of how much there is to hurt
them, in themselves and outside themselves; aching in his
wish that they maintain integrity and a decent Family
loyalty. He has influenced thousands of poets: Black
poets, Hispanic poets, and strangely, you may feel,
Caucasian poets, who sensed a vibrance, a vigor in his
dealings with language which they came to admire.

Haki has said: "What writers write about tells to
what extent they are involved with the real world. Bad
writing containing the most 'revolutionary' idea is, first

and last, <u>bad writing</u>. A high standard must be met if the writer is to communicate effectively. The ability to develop a style that is clear, original, and communicative is what separates writers from non-writers."

Haki, ten years ago, had a famous list of Black cliches he wanted to see in Black poetry NOT AGAIN. I think he would endorse that list today!

warrior	pride
ebony	soul
whitey	universe
Queen of the Nile	cosmos
right on!	nigger
<u>African warrior</u>	genocide
pig	vibrations
	Black is Beautiful
	revolution
	respect
	change!

Here is Haki Madhubuti (<u>pssst:</u> AFRICAN WARRIOR!)

YEVGENY YEVTUSHENKO

He is a poet I've saluted ever since I met him, about 1962, in a Frank Lloyd Wright home in Libertyville, Illinois. Because he is a truth-teller.

I was introduced to Yevgeny Yevtushenko by an unjustly obscure Alabama-born Chicago critic, the late Van Allen Bradley. Said Van Allen to Yevgeny, out there on the Libertyville veranda of Kathryn Lewis -- "Want you to meet this gr-reat writer." He handed Yevgeny my book "Annie Allen." Yevgeny stood soberly in the bright Libertyville sunshine, soberly turned pages -- and soberly said -- what he was s'posed to say. Voznesensky was there, too; and other Russian writers.

What has stayed in my memory all these years is the poignant picture those vivid, vibrant, shy AND sly young Russian mischiefs made in the back of the bus that bounced us away from that estate. They were all singing beautiful Russian songs, and the most fervent of them all was ZHENYA (he told me to say "ZHENYA"). I can still see him, sitting in the direct, cradling sunshine, singing with this half-sly, half-shy, winkful lustiness. He drew all of us bus people into the gentle rowdyness of his celebration. He looked at me and winked as he sang. As a rule, I hate winks. A wink is almost always an ineffectual wishful aim at sophistication. But this wink was fresh, and honest, and sadly wise -- and young and old and innocently merry.

I salute the creator of that Salvation of a poem, "Babiy Yar": I salute this creator of such warm influences as "Weddings", "Talking", and that little jewel, "Cowards Have Small Possibilities", "Zima

Junction"; and "A Precocious Autobiography," which, brilliant and brave, has been for me a variety of School.

KERI HULME

The Pegasus Prize for Maori Literature was awarded to "The Bone People" in July of 1984, after a committee of distinguished scholars selected it from the best Maori novels, stories, <u>and</u> autobiographies written in a decade. It won also the 1984 New Zealand Book Award.

The author, Keri Hulme, is the author of poetry, non-fiction, and a forthcoming collection of short stories, but "The Bone People" is her first novel.

Keri Hulme -- she says of herself -- is particular about "the <u>shape</u> of words." She subscribes to "oddities, ... experiments, and eccentricities." "The Bone People" is "passing strange", she assures you, like the original mouthful of <u>kina roe</u>. "PERSIST! Kina can become a favorite food."

She is very funny when she writes <u>about</u> her book. I like her sassy instruction: "Make of it what you will."

Keri Hulme pounds, punches, stabs, gallops, stomps, skips, stumbles, winks and bewitches. The life she depicts is chiefly raw. I mean that Keri Hulme, although her book is jewelled, is impatient with ornament for ornament's sake, and with rigid design; she is impatient with anything less than the purity of honest revelation. She is boldly slangy. There is a loose splendor about the irreverent poetry romping through her prose.

Once you have read "The Bone People", I believe, it will be difficult to forget the colloquial heroine, artist Kerewin Holmes. Large-souled, she wants to mend the world-wound. She resents and scorns, she loves, she extends herself. She spits and studies her spit with interest and philosophy. She drinks lots of beer. She smokes cigarillos, she enjoys a pipe. In a bar, she says "Wonder what would happen if I started singing out loud?" In telling her that she may have stomach cancer, a doctor speaks to her bluntly, speaks to her as though she were an idiot child. She replies to him in kind! -- and adds "You are getting beyond yourself, little medicine man." (Wouldn't we all love to say that.)

We have here, also, two other main characters, a mute affectionate boy named Simon, and his stepfather Joe, volcanic and tender by turns. But it is Kerewin who strides impudently in, to establish and certify her deserved place in the literature of the world.

I hope Keri Hulme feels free to <u>give</u> herself to you tonight. Like her book, she is a warm wild woman -- and you will love her.

MARI EVANS

Mari Evans does not feel that it is important for you to know how many years her beauty has graced the earth, nor whether or not her mother wore organdy and lace on old-time Sunday afternoons, nor whether or not her father bought her cotton candy at the church bazaar or the amusement park, nor whether or not she saw her dentist a week ago Wednesday afternoon. You have your programs so you know where she has taught and what she has written. You are about to hear her deliver her poetry.

Although Mari is headquartered in Indiana, she is richly known and revered in Detroit, Chicago, Los Angeles, Milwaukee, Philadelphia. And in all these places, she is known as a "Queen of Africa." In a few moments you'll have <u>some</u> notion of why this honor is hers. She has dignity, warm composure, clear sincerity, <u>vast</u> knowledges, pride in what she is, a radiant understanding of what she is.

Critic Richard Long has said "She speaks in the tone and idiom of urban Black folk, and with biting wit probes the paradoxes of Black American Life."

JAMES BALDWIN

You know the phrase "larger than life." If that
phrase is valid at all, it likes James Baldwin.

This man has dared to confront and examine himself,
ourselves, and the enigmas between.

Many have been called prophets but here is a BONA
FIDE prophet. Long ago he guaranteed "The fire next time!
No more water: the FIRE next time!"

Virtually the following day we, smelling smoke, looked
out, and found ourselves surrounded by leering, singing
fire. I wonder how many others have regarded this
connection. AND NO!! James Baldwin did NOT start a fire:
he Foretold its coming. He was a PRE-REPORTER. He was
a PROPHET.

His friends enjoy calling him Jimmy -- and that is
easy to understand. The man is love personified. He has a
sweet, softly loving, endearing smile. (Smile, Jimmy.) He
has a voice that can range from eerie, effortless menace -
- menace educational and creative -- to this low, cradling,
insinuating and involving love. This love is at once both
father and son to a massive concern -- a concern for his

own people, <u>surely</u>, but for the <u>cleansing</u>, the <u>extension, of</u> <u>all</u> the world's categories no less <u>surely</u>; since he knows - - SURELY -- that the fortunes of These Over Here affect, inevitably, the fortunes of Those Over There.

Essayist, novelist, poet, playwright, new French Legion of Honor Medalist, human being being <u>HUMAN</u>—

James Baldwin.

GARRISON KEILLOR

Jenny Rutland, our non-stop, deep, funny, bright-as-a-new-penny associate in the Poetry Office, who has long loved Garrison Keillor, was marveling over this Impending Visit.

"What do <u>you</u> think accounts for his great fame?"

I answered, approximately: "He's the fella next door, that we think we know so well -- but suspect, in our <u>abler</u> ruminations, that we do not know so well. He <u>is</u> special, and since we almost reluctantly <u>understand</u> that, we are willing to let him display to us <u>himself</u> and <u>ourselves!</u>"

What revelations in Garrison Keillor's pages. What portraits. What lightning in the center of BREAD. Or, again, what little sudden piquant insights. You <u>yearn</u> to

quote them. You <u>yearn</u> to sing that high school song,
beginning "Hail to <u>thee</u>, Lake Wobegon, the cradle of our
youth. . . . .

> We shall uphold
> the blue and gold
> in honor and in truth . . . . ."

Certain writers are characterized by particular
powers and graces. Even though their subjects may be
similar to the subjects of others, <u>if they are daring</u> --
(and a writer who wants to be truthful, who wants to
Reach, has got to be daring) -- their animating hands upon
clay are absolutely like <u>no other</u> hands upon clay.
<u>There</u>fore, ONLY Melvin Van Peebles can introduce you to
"Lillie", in "Br'er Soul," and assure you that "Lillie
Done the Zampoughi ev' <u>time</u> I pull huh coat-tail." (And
<u>demonstrate</u>!) And only Garrison Keillor has introduced
you to Uncle Senator K. Thorvaldson. And here I quote
briefly: "Who else has a great-uncle named Senator?
How do you explain to people that he was named that
because his mother liked the sound of it? If he was
normal it might be okay, but he's even battier than the
others." End quote.

<u>Wups</u>. After jotting <u>that</u> down, I'm remembering:
_____ Long ago, bef<u>ore</u> this day of easy and "accepted"
familiarity, Blacks in the old South didn't appreciate
whites calling grown-<u>up</u> Blacks by their first names, so

many named their children Captain, Major, Colonel, Squire, Duke, King, Highness and LORD (That drove many a poor "master" wild OR to an unwilling courtesy.)

Well, here to get you giggling and gulping is Garrison Keillor.

KOFI AWOONOR

Kofi Awoonor appears here on a history day -- January 20, 1986, the first national Martin Luther King celebration day. I am sure Mr. Awoonor feels the honor of the Library's special choosing. And of course he deserves it.

All and any African writers -- African French, African English, African American, African African -- are unified by one powerful persuasion: the desire to avoid enslavement.

Out and promenading, cleanly promenading, or maybe just under a confusion of contradictory images, or maybe (sadly) DEEP down, or maybe braided through an offended consciousness -- is the profound desire NOT to be a slave, NOT to be enslaved.

You'll be aware of this truth whether you are listening to the frankly "political" Gil Scott Heron, or,

listening to the honeyed pugilism of Aime Cesaire --
(quote) "My memory is circled with blood. My memory is
girdled with corpses;" or, listening to the unrelentingly
"craft"-conscious Leopold Sedar Senghor, of Senegal; or,
listening to ardent Leon Damas --
(quote) --

>   "I feel like an awful fool
>   accomplice among them
>   panderer among them
>   cut-throat among them
>   my hands hideously red
>   with the blood of their
>   ci-vi-li-zation";
or, listeniing to the incisively lush David Diop: (quote)

>   "You who bend you who weep
>   You who die one day just like that
>   not knowing why
>   You who struggle and stay awake for
>   the Other's rest
>   You with no more laughter in your look
>   You my brother with face of fear and
>   anguish
>   Rise and shout: NO!"

or, listening to South African Dennis Brutus -- who has
been imprisoned, who has been carefully tortured -- but is

<u>still</u> able to say, be<u>yond</u> his concern for elegant lyricism, (quote)

> "Somehow we survive,
> and tenderness, frustrated, does not
> wither."

or, <u>finally</u>, listening to Kofi Awoonor say what <u>he</u> is <u>going</u> to say immediately after I tell you that Kofi Awoonor is richly prized for <u>his</u> frank interest in freedom, for his <u>positive</u> pictures of disintegration, for his <u>physical faith</u> in (quote) "the feast of oneness whose ritual we partook of."

Kofi Awoonor.

GENERAL INTRODUCTION TO THE POETRY
SOCIETY OF AMERICA'S PRESENTATION
OF SIX POETS: BARBARA GUEST,
MICHAEL HARPER, DAVID IGNATOW,
GRACE SCHULMAN, GALWAY KINNELL
LOUIS SIMPSON

Sometimes I feel that much of today's poetry, chopped journalism, with negligible spice here and there, is doomed to be attended only by its manufacturers. (Of course, there are so many of those you might be reflecting that's quite a hefty audience in itself.)

This fear does not mean I am requiring the return of the spirit of Edgar A. Guest. No. Nor the return of the valid spirit-hands of Gerard Manley Hopkins, Robert Frost, Paul Valery, Arthur Rimbaud, Alex Pope, T.S. Eliot and Papa Pound, Robert Lowell, Dickinson, Donne, Dylan. Nor the spirit-hand of the author of "The Twa Corbies" -- (which is perfectly lovely.) Nor do I require that poetry be "understood" -- in the general understanding of that word "understood."

_____ Well -- we are in no real danger (we reverencers of poetry) as long as these Six, and other poets with their integrity, their self-respect, their loyalty to language and to life, continue to practice, continue to experiment, continue to be UNAFRAID of prune-souled spankers. <u>They</u> re<u>fuse</u> to number themselves among the crowd of frightened yay-saying viewers of the invisibility of The Emperor's Clothes. And they re<u>fuse</u> to commit the utter sin -- the MAJOR CRIME -- of being Deadly Dull.

BARBARA GUEST

I don't know if she lives there now, but she has been <u>described</u> as living on Long Island "with sky, sea, clouds, and great silences." Many of us could envy her that shining, <u>forming</u> circumstance. "Seeking Air" is her novel, and significant books of poems are "Moscow Mansions," "The Countess From Minneapolis."

Barbara Guest has an excitingly efficient control over her rhythms, which are subtle riders -- (she is unqualifiedly a musician!) -- and her painter's images, which make me think, a little, of Toi Derricotte.

I don't know if she is a painter or not; but one is likely to su<u>rmise</u>, reading her poems, that she could turn smoothly from pen and page to paint-pot and brush and canvas.

Barbara Guest.

MICHAEL HARPER

Michael Harper believes that delight is possible for the reader as well as the creator of poetry, believes that the reader — when permitted — participates in the act of creation — <u>extending</u>, often, this wonder of <u>making</u>—within the limits, of course, of individual experience and fantasy.

Well, Michael Harper is right there to cooperate with this <u>need</u> of the reader. Further, in much of his poetry he has defied the orthodox, the alien, the prescribed, the timid and the dim. His work with language is various and respectful.

Here is the author of the classic "A Mother Speaks: The Algiers Motel Incident, Detroit", and of other shapely and persuasive excellences.

Michael Harper.

DAVID IGNATOW

Not regularly is he jounced about by critics-with-crowns: perhaps because they don't know quite what to make of him. Here is this man, ambling forth, saying things that have the impact of simplicity: and for heaven's sake! -- (ours, <u>too</u>) -- the simplicity turns out to be intelligent. (That's almost forbidden.) The simplicity turns out to be wise. (That's almost PUNISHABLE.) The simplicity turns out to be -- medical. The simplicity turns out to be -- not so simple always.

I have met David Ignatow once before today. We read on the same afternoon, in a campus program. Before the readings, we had a chance to talk. Only the one hour was necessary to assure me that I was in the company of a remarkable intellect. I had decided already that his poetry was exceptional: funny, chilling, igniting, frightened, brave. Human. (Stop being scared of that word.)

David Ignatow.

GRACE SCHULMAN

Even when Grace Schulman's poems are short, and the lines narrow, we have the impression that we are at the center of large sound -- large, exacting but involving sound. Her rhythms are obliged and reliable: so remarkable is her control that you feel confident and comfortable leaning into those rhythms.

Her frequent pentameter is brilliantly leashed and various. That pentameter is never tiresome.

Also: the people and circumstances she tackles are real. They are not static.

She is not static.

Grace Schulman.

GALWAY KINNELL

Galway Kinnell once spoke of the "greatness of creating a poem anew as you read it." (He was talking about poets reading their poems to audiences.) He didn't say this always happens. He wanted you to understand that it is "great" when it does happen.

Listen tonight for proofs of the following passionate Kinnellian beliefs: a. that the ultimate resources of the English language should be available to poets — and, indeed, to all of us as daily arrangers of language. To lose any of — I quote — "the gorgeous words of the English language seems a waste." (End quote.) b. that "we belong to life in the same way as do the other animals and the plants and stones." End quote. c. that we (human beings) are not super, but "evolutionary." d. I quote Galway: "I think involvement in the effort to alleviate pain in the world, whether a militant cause, or just caring for a sick person, any involvement at all which seeks justice and brings you into a feeling of love and community, is purifying and is bound to be nourishing -- and this is true whether you are a writer or not."

Galway Kinnell.

LOUIS SIMPSON

"Something Wicked This Way Comes."
Here comes Louis Simpson -- communicator of intricate darkness of feeling and instinct (so says Donald Hall); fiery defender of Gary Snyder; accused Universalist. Certain circles cite him as coldly capable of <u>exhaustive</u> wickedness. For almost two decades he has been soundly spanked for opining that, if Blacks write "<u>only</u>" about Blackness, they are inadequate -- that they are, in fact, non-poets. You decide for yourselves whether or not <u>that's</u> wicked. But I myself found out how dangerous Simpson the Satyr can be. I remember with delight that years ago, at Stonybrook, I was having a lovely peaceful lunch with this remarkable poet and teacher in a cheerfully sunny room, when I made the mistake of saying that there were no Gr-r-reat Poets -- Capital G, Capital P -- living and writing today. (That we <u>knew</u> of, that is: because of course there is Always some unknown genius toiling at the top of a tenement, about to

burst -- full-bodied and beautiful and persuasive -- upon the populace.) "No Great Poets? GARY SNYDER!" screamed Louis. Louis turned red -- he can do that -- and, lifting himself to hellish height in his chair, bit my head off. (That is why I have no head. . .)

Oh well, wicked or not, Louis Simpson, poet of careful subjectivity, poet of luminous, requiring lyricism, is here tonight.

PEN_____

PATRICIA McCONNEL
JOYCE CAROL OATES
LES MURRAY
W.D. WETHERELL
JOHN TAGLIABUE
MICHAEL BENEDIKT

PATRICIA McCONNEL

In Winifred Oglethorpe, Patricia McConnel has given us a character I hope will be continued. I can see a bookful of stories, or a novel, about the lover of life you are going to meet.

Patricia McConnel blends woe and wit and wonder with apparent ease. Her pen is not intense. Her pen, or typewriter, prefers a genial balance to stiff self-consciousness.

Sometimes we forget what made the classics classic. The classics are interesting. Aristotle, Confucius, Chaucer, Dante, Bacon, Pushkin, Thackeray, Shakespeare, W.E.B. DuBois ___ all are interesting. Machiavelli is devilishly INTERESTING. Who knows what the Ages will say about this new achiever, the interesting Patricia McConnel.

JOYCE CAROL OATES

Joyce Carol Oates for many years has given you palpable people, moving through sophisticated agitation, or fright that is never simple, or joy that misses radiance, or solutions that leave the problem triumphant. Her flexible harmonies of language and of understanding have always paid court to one another.

The story she reads tonight will impress you with its contemporary pertinence and chill.

LES MURRAY

Australian Les Murray has said that he is interested in "patterns of life and their meaning".

In his work you will find a genial devotion to rural Australia, to the stabilities of tradition, to maintenance of what is fine and strong in his homeland.

Les Murray has said that he has written "mainly out of love for a difficult ancient art," and "to interest, challenge and delight" his readers. He speaks warmly of "the joy and the rituals" of writing poetry. "You <u>have</u> to do it!" he exclaims, but it works only if you do it for others as well as for yourself. Theoretical systems, he feels, "try to limit art, to interpret it down to some level where it can be fitted into specific ways of thinking. This serves the purposes of social-climbing rather than of art," he says, "and will probably always be around, but we need not take it too seriously." (I quote.)

From the glorious to the absurd Les Murray travels. His poetry is frank and energetic. He is forthright. Clarity and coherence are two of his advantages. Humor and mischief are two more.

After observing Les Murray at lunch, I went back to the Jefferson Building and wrote:

Oh, Poet !

You with your sprightly wilfulness,
your animated shimmer, your
shadows and sunlit places, your
stylish joy___
your dedication to the daily,
your fierce affinities, your fond dismay,
your perceptions of drama in the so-called Small --
I observe you! and I credit you!
I pass you on!
I yield you to your Neighbor!

W.D. WETHERELL

Reading this author's story, I remembered that Isaac Bashevis Singer said "literature must <u>describe events</u>, not analyze ideas."

W.D. Wetherell may or may not like the sound or sense of that, as YOU may or may not -- but it is true indeed that he can and wants to <u>describe events</u> with a jolly skill that keeps the captive involved.

At <u>least</u> the justly loved Mr. Singer did <u>not</u> order you to come out of a story idea-less.

<u>You</u> decide whether or not Mr. Wetherell is subtly--or stealthily--analyzing any ideas.

W.D. Wetherell

JOHN TAGLIABUE

The music of John Tagliabue is magnetizing. I could say that it <u>lulls</u>, were it not for the fact that it is protein-rich and therefore renders you soldier-sharp!

There is an aching subscription to traditional sanities in this poetry. It is informed by the poet's delight in wide experience of the world; for this poet has reached and has been reached by many lands. But what is foreign has never possessed him. <u>Nothing</u> possesses him. You are not surprised to learn that Mark Van Doren was one of John Tagliabue's early technical and spiritual compulsions: but he took off from Van Doren with impatient though reverential impudence. I say with semi-reluctant mischief: he had other fish to fry.

Well, he has provided for us haunting perfumes from long ago, sharp awareness of contemporary beauty <u>and</u> rascality; he has provided a muscular lyricism.

MICHAEL BENEDIKT

Sprightly -- saying what you may not have expected the poet to say, using jauntinesses you have not anticipated. That's Michael Benedikt, pedestrian unexpectedly, air-borne unexpectedly: in <u>any</u> of these certainties <u>taking you with him</u>.

This is the clown, with one eye mourning.

This is W.C. Fields -- with <u>deference</u> (sometimes.)

This is a "native New Yorker." Without being instructed, you might suppose <u>that</u>, early on.

How Benediktian that, in his own little smudged resume, he'll tell you that he was Poetry Editor of the Paris Review from 1978 to 1974.

How Benediktian that, tongue-in-cheek, he laments; and that, tear-in-eye, he laughs to beat the band.

I think he will give you a whopping good time.

Michael Benedikt.

FAMILY PICTURES

Then there's li'l Ms. Entrepreneur.
She be a ticket-and-a-half.
I mean, she take you way past where you want to go.

Then there's Satin-Legs Smith. In his Sundays.
Below the tinkling trade of little coins
the gold impulse not possible to show.
Or spend. Promise piled over and betrayed.

In the Mecca
Aunt Dill extends
sinister pianissimos and apples,
and at that moment of the Thousand Souls is
a Christ-like creature, Doing Good.

Then there's Malcolm ....
(in a soft and fundamental hour
a sorcery devout and vertical
beguiled the world.)

Then there's
an Old Black Woman, Homeless, and indistinct.
Folks used to celebrate your birthday!
Folks used to say "She's such a pretty little thing!"

Folks used to say "She draws such handsome horses,
        cows, and houses!"
Folks used to say "That child is going <u>far</u>!"

Then there's Boy Breaking Glass: "I shall create! If not a
                                note, a hole.
If not an overture, a desecration...............
...........Nobody knew where I was, and now I am no longer
there."

I GIVE YOU MY GALLERY.

    So many boys. Boys. Lincoln West. Merle. Ulysses.
Shabaka. Martin D. The Near-Johannesburg Boy. Diego.
Kojo. Seven boys in a pool room during schooltime. The
Pool Players, Seven at The Golden Shovel —

                We real cool. We
                Left school. We

                Lurk late. We
                Strike straight. We

                Sing sin. We
                Thin gin. We

                Jazz June. We
                Die soon.

Die soon. Today, many such boys -- their girl friends, too -- EXPECT to "die soon." In Chicago. In New York. In Springfield, in Philadelphia. In Whatalotago, Alabama. In Detroit. (In Washington D.C.?) They do not expect to become twenty-one. They are designing their funerals. Their caskets will be lined with Kente cloth. They choose their music: they want rap, they want Queen Latifah.

Girls. Girls. Late Annie, Little 'Bout-town Gal, Sadie and Maud. The hunchback girl. Gang Girls. Tinsel Marie. Novelle. Laini Nzinga. And the little girl who believes we have a Right to sing.

See men. Men who are prisoners. See stunted men. See men reaching. Matthew Cole, who rooms in a stove-heated flat, over on Lafayette. School-teacher Alfred. Here's a Garbageman. Here are Langston Hughes and Paul Robeson. The Preacher ruminates behind the sermon. Soldiers. The Soft Man. Uncle Seagram. A Man of the Middle Class; here is A song of A Man of the Middle Class:

> I'm what has gone out blithely and with noise
> Returning! I'm what rushed around to pare
> Down rind, to find fruit frozen under there.
>
> I am bedraggled, with sundry dusts to be shed;
> Trailing desperate tarnished tassels. These
> strident Aprils
> With terrifying polkas and Bugle Calls
> Confound me.

_____ Although I've risen! and my back is bold.
My tongue is brainy, choosing from among
Care, rage, surprise, despair, and choosing care.
I'm semi-splendid within what I've defended.

Yet, there I totter, there limp laxly. My
Uncomely trudge
To Plateau That and platitudinous Plateau
Whichever is no darling to my grudge-choked
Industry or usual alcohol.

I've roses to guard
In the architectural prettiness of my yard.
(But there are no paths remarkable for
Wide believable welcomes.)

I have loved directions.
I have loved orders and an iron to stride, I,
Whose hands are papers now,
Fit only for tossing in this outrageous air.

Not God nor grace nor candy balls
Will get me everything different and the same!

My wife has canvas walls.

My wife never quite forgets to put flowers in vases,
Bizarre prints in the most unusual places,
Give teas for poets, wear odoriferous furs.
An awful blooming is hers.

I've antique firearms. Blackamoors. Chinese
Rugs, ivories.
Bronzes. Everything I Wanted.
But have I answers? Oh methinks
I've answers such as have
The executives I copied long ago,
The ones who, forfeiting Vicks salve,
Prayer book and Mother, shot themselves last Sunday.
All forsaking

All that was theirs but for their money's taking.

I've answers such as Giants used to know.
There's a Giant who'll jump next Monday; all forsaking
Wives, safes and solitaire
And the elegant statue standing at the foot of the stair.

Women. Women. <u>Besides</u> li'l Ms. Entrepreneur. I give
you Maud Martha. Pearl May Lee. The mother of Emmett
Till. Winnie Mandela. Mrs. Small. Annie Allen. Hattie
Scott. Queen of the Blues. Those of my sisters who kept
their naturals. Women, <u>yes</u>. Some with no hallelujahs, no
hurrahs at all, no handshakes. I can say, to numbers of
these women,

There remain large countries in your eyes.
Shrewd sun.
The civil balance.
The listening secrets.

And you create and train your flowers still.

All the aforementioned are among my Family Pictures. "Family Pictures" is the title of a book of my poetry, published in 1970. "Family" therein referred to is Blackness.

Blackness is what I know very well. Of course, we Blacks know much about <u>whites</u>. As I said to a bevy of those, back in 1951, "We know the condition of your gums because we have been so long between your teeth." That remains an appropriate judgment in this seventy-sixth of my years.

Indeed, however, Blackness is what I know best. I want to talk about it, with definitive illustration, in this time when hostility between races intensifies and swirls; in this time when numbers of Blacks detest themselves and announce that detestation with amazing and multiplying audacity; when hordes of Black men and women straighten their hair and bleach their complexions and narrow their noses and spell their eyes light gray or green or cerulean -- thereby announcing: What nature afforded is poor, is sub-standard, is inferior to Caucasian glory.

Several years ago a lovely actress announced "I don't FEEL Black. In fact, I'm really <u>blue</u> -- the color of consciousness."

I accept a once-spanked Decision, that old legislation. If you have "One Drop" of Blackness blood in you -- yes, of COURSE it comes out red!--you are mine. You are a member of my Family. (Oh, mighty Drop.)

I have the liveliest interest in _other_ families. I believe that we should _all_ know each other, we human carriers of so many pleasurable differences. To not-know is to doubt, to shrink from, side-step, or destroy.

Hear that phrase: 'pleasurable differences.' How boring would be a world rife with roses only. I cite, applaud not only roses, but dandelions, daisies and tulips, geraniums, honeysuckle, a violet, jonquils -- and Black Orchids. Each flower-family is valid, respectable, unabridged. I do not believe that daisies want to be daffodils, tulips or roses or peacocks or crocodiles.

Our People. We _commence_ from the concept of _our_-ness. Our people. I use the phrase often. When that phrase is used by Hispanics, Koreans, Chinese, Japanese, Jews, Native Americans, nobody snorts, nobody sneers. When a Black uses the phrase "our people," _much_ of listening blood -- _not_ all, but _much_ of listening blood-- begins to roil and boil, and the poor Black affirmer is likely to be called a racist, an affirmer of _racism_. How can _that_ be? Racism is prejudice _with_ oppression. That is: you have a right to loathe your neighbor's green eyes.

But your revulsion must not persuade you to scrape those green eyes out of their nests.

I put my Family Pictures on the wall. Numbers of Family turn away, preferring to "worship" elsewhere, otherwise. A few years ago a Black maiden assured me: "I don't care WHAT happens to the Blaaa-ack Race." She, on a chiefly white campus, was president of her Black Student Union. "I'm not Black," she said, her ebony face tensing. "My mother comes from Haiti." Hmmmm......Earlier, she had objected fiercely to my recitation of "The Life of Lincoln West," a poem presenting a small Black boy coming to terms with outdoor and indoor opinions of his identity.

More often than not, when I speak of Blackness, I'm asked a challenging question: "BUT! -- are you or are you not an American? -- Don't you feel American?" "Oh, yes!" I answer. "Yes."

On Being An American: In America you feel a little or a lot disoriented, so far as "being Black-and-being-an-American" goes! In the last few decades many citizens have adopted a resistance to adoration of country. And true, a country that for so long endorsed slavery, endorsed lynching, endorsed official segregation, and could be capable of judging scholarly rejection acceptable is not to be blue-ribboned across the board.

But traveling to other countries helps you italicize American positives. Once you get out of the country, whatever your woes, your wobblinesses, your confusions, your furies, you understand that you are <u>operationally</u> an American.

I myself am forced to realize that I am <u>claimed</u> by no other country. (<u>My</u> kind <u>is</u> claimed by this country, albeit reluctantly.) Furthermore, traveling teaches you that cruelty and superposing are everywhere.

Although it is not true that calling myself an American will instantly protect me from harm or detention <u>any</u>where in the world -- when I was a little girl I thought this was true -- still that <u>concept</u> of a large arm to lean on is implicit. <u>Implicit</u>: do not make plans to do any leaning.

It is not so easy for an "American" to abstain from "being an American." However roots-proud you as a Black may be, when asked "What are you?" in Dublin, Devon, London, Lyon, Israel, Iran, Ghana, in Moscow or Madrid, it is expedient and "natural" to reply, <u>twinge</u>lessly, "American." Because your questioner is impatient. Your questioner is ready for the Definer behind you. Your questioner has small time -- and <u>no</u> time for your efforts at self-clarification.

Back to my American <u>Challenger</u>. Having decided that I am not <u>too</u> sinful, that I <u>am</u> allowing myself to be called "American", that Challenger has another query for me. "But! -- what about <u>humanitarianism?</u> Are you not humanitarian?" "Yes." "You call yourself a Black. Doesn't that singularization fight the concept of humanitarianism?"

OF COURSE I am "concerned," tightly, "with human welfare and the reduction of suffering." I cite, star, and esteem all that which is of woman - human and hardly human. And I want the people of the world to anticipate ultimate unity, <u>active</u> interest in empathy. I commend a unity of distinct proud pieces. Not a Stew. A <u>unity</u> of distinct proud pieces. Because each entity is lovely -- amazing -- <u>exhilarating</u> in uniquity and boldness of clear distinction, good design. I hope that in the world, always, there will be Black, brown, yellow, white, red. (And if Time has some surprises for us let us welcome those too.)

_____<u>None</u> of this -- this interest <u>in</u> and subscription <u>to</u> ALL -- can ever turn me from my healthy concern for my Black Extension. It hurts me that so many members of that Extension would rather be anything <u>but</u> Black. There is this hulking inner nervousness when the word Black is heard. As I said some time ago, and find myself repeating, it is the kind of nervousness that sends <u>throngs</u> of Blacks running to the currently popular "security" (quotes! quotes!) of the phrase "African-American," a phrase now self-consciously beginning to invade our literature. What, in the next fifty years, can this mean to our Black lives, our Black literature and launch?

FAMILYHOOD. The current motion to make the phrase "African-American" an official identification is cold and excluding. What of our Family members in Ghana? -- in Tanzania? -- in Kenya? -- in Nigeria? -- in South Africa? -- in Brazil? Why are we pushing them out of our consideration? -- out of our concern.

The capitalized names Black and Blacks were appointed to comprise an open, sensitizing, wide-stretching, unifying, empowering umbrella.

Some Blacks announce "That name Black does not describe all of us." Does the name "white" describe all of the people claiming its services? Those skins are yellow and rose and cocoa and cream and pink and gray and scarlet, and rust and purple and taupe and tan. Ecru. But that word "white," to those who wear it, is sacrosanct, is to be guarded, cherished. My beside-the-bed dictionary says: Caucasian -- a member of the light-skinned division (get that: division) of humanity.

With my own little Kojo in "Children Coming Home" I assert:

I am other than Hyphenation.

. . . .

I am a Black . . . .
And I capitalize my name.
Do not call me out of my name.

This objection of mine to the designation African-
American is not popular. Nevertheless! The phase is
ISLANDING. The phrase is limiting. The phrase is weak.
Today's popularization is very sly: the appellation comes
already capitalized. That detail appeals to many Blacks.
The Black spirit, the Black fighting spirit, like any other
spirit, sometimes gets tired.

The Black spirit fought so painfully to get "colored"
capitalized, and "Negro" capitalized, and Black capitalized.
Newspapers and magazines, in referring to Black people as
Blacks, still refuse to honor the notion of respectable and
respected identity, and insist on spelling Blacks with a
little "b." The tiredness of the Black spirit has noted this,
and with glee has noted also that "African-American"
comes all capitalized (no fight involved) and that white
people, although much amused by the entire Little Fray,
seem disposed to accept it, this soft-sounding sanction,
albeit with a little paternalistic head-shaking. "Tsk tsk.
What will these weird little creatures think of next? Odd.
Bizarre. But at least, no offensiveness here. Almost a
honeyed music: AF-ri-can A-MER-i-can." (As opposed to
B-L-A-C-K ! Which comes right out to meet you, eye to
eye.)

THE BLACK FAMILY! I speak now of the little unit within the large Extension. My brother and I were fortunate. Growing up in a home in which Blackness was cleanly honored -- valued -- allowed us peace and range. I still exclaim, as I exclaimed in 1989, I know very well that there are Black weaknesses, Black failings, and fallings-off. But numbers of us ache for balance in these contemporary reports. Numbers of us claim views, prominent views, of amiable Black Family, morally nourished Black Family, nice Black Family. Yes, Blacks are involved in drug abuse and drug-dealing, and alcoholism and pill-popping, and theft and assault and child-desertion and prostitution and homicide; as are whites, browns, reds, yellows. But there are also the firm families: the durable, effective and forward youngsters; the homes regularized and rich with intelligence, affection, communication and merriment. The necessary corrective programs must flourish -- individual, state, national, world. But the already-successes must be announced, featured, credited.

My husband, Henry Blakely, a writer and social planner, is in this company with our brilliant daughter, theatre-founder Nora Brooks Blakely. We have a brilliant son, California software designer Henry the Third. Henry the Second and I were married fifty-five years ago. In the Black community, many long-lasting marriages jog along, jog along. Rarely do these hit the headlines. The headlines are reserved for the teen-aged unmarried mother: rarely the manymanymanymany lovely young girls who are clean-willed, cleanly adventurous, warm of heart and clear of spirit: reasonable, sane young girls, in love with the ideals of knowledge, good citizenship.

Indeed, who is to guarantee that such positives have eluded every one of the teen-aged unmarried mothers? Incidentally: the loud critics of teen-aged unmarried mothers and of one-parent homes are not considering the amount of pain they are lavishing on innocent children who happen to be members of single-parented homes. Are such keen and sly-tongued assessors aware of the permanent harm they are inflicting on these children -- of the hot contribution they are making to loss of self-esteem? Do they want to contribute to that loss? Do they want to inspire innumerable playground comparison-conversations: "I'm better'n you, because I have a double-parented home. I'm better'n better'n better'n you." Cheerily ignored is the truth that an impressive percentage of double-parented homes -- and I include the most luxurious Caucasian homes -- are hell-holes of sexual abuse, child-beating, wife-battering, bickering, incessant profanity, elegant drug-dealing, pornography-exposition, racism-espousal. Left out of current diatribes are recipes these single mothers really could use. Questions come to mind. How do you force a man to stay in the home -- thus maintaining "double-parenting." How do you force a man's society-weakened body to stay alive? -- thus maintaining the supposed efficiency of double-parenting. When a husband dies, the home is no longer double-parented. Are the then-fatherless children in that home automatically doomed to failure and moral depravity? Proud double-parented homers on Monday, after the death on Tuesday or Thursday are they to hang their little heads in shame? -- in kindergarten? -- on the playground? -- because they are now dimmed, maimed, permanently demoted citizens of that horror of horrors, the Infamous, insecure, ugly disgrace, the SINGLE-PARENTED home.

Franklin Roosevelt experienced a single-parented home. Abraham Lincoln experienced a single-parented home. Angela Lansbury experienced a single-parented home.

The Black Community! Recovery? Repair? Revival? Unhappily, I'm obliged to subscribe to the Long View. There will be no abrupt cessation of The Summer Killings, nor of those in fall and winter and spring. Unless there rises, with seeming suddenness, a Loved Leader, who, like Malcolm X, advised of upset in a certain New York vicinity, could proceed to that vicinity with still face and straight backbone, raise -- not a fist! -- a single open hand, thus putting instant finish to the unpleasantness. I do not predict such a visitation. Think: is there anyone today who is significantly adored? Yes, there are little bowings and scrapings here and there, in this sub-community and that sub-community. But not one among High Lords or High Ladies has been able, on a grand scale, to put an end to murder, assault, cripplings, chaos. (And we all know what happened to Malcolm, Martin, Medgar.)

Indeed, the Enthroning Time may be done. There may be no further Malcolms or Martins or Medgars to be shot off their ascensions. We Blacks (finally) may have to give up any lingering wish to put all our burdens and decision-making potential into the hands of one supreme individual. We may have to think for ourselves, validate ourselves, defend ourselves. Of course, some aspect of committee will be indicated! (Some assume there must be committee in heaven!) We'll ALWAYS have to risk faith in committee. Committee created not out of reverence, in the conference room, for an exhibition of fine gray wool, poisonous earrings or skirts above the bony knee, but out of deserved respect for seriousness, sanity, good will, and absolute non-sleaze. Respect by Blacks for Blackness.

Pointing to a contemporary welt, I say what may startle: I am acquainted with many lovable Jews! In so far as I know, not one Jew has marauded or personally minimized me. That is <u>my</u> story. Others must speak out of their own experience.

I deplore blanket detestation of any group. See "Fiddler On The Roof," ye who believe that liking Jews is impossible. If your eyes aren't in trouble when Tevye sings to his sweetly taut and testy wife "Do you love me?" -- if your chest isn't chained when he chats with his God, shrugs, jokes with his God, grimaces, and finally, in a time of "abrupt" affliction, affliction that comes across as totally ridiculous and crazily cruel, merely spreads his palms <u>at</u> the sky, at his God --- WELL! -- cold Brothers, cold Sisters, cold Cousins! I must title you "Infected"; I must title you Terminal.

All haters of Blacks, of Blackness -- see Alex Haley's "Roots." I believe that most cannot experience it and remain haters of Blacks, Blackness. See the father, forcing the gaze of his infant son toward the sky, and announcing, as he lifts the little body high, **BEHOLD**: the **ON**ly thing greater than yourself. _____Whether you're religious or not, whether you believe or do not believe that God lives at 444 West Heaven-town, if your eyes and throat and chest aren't in trouble when you experience <u>that</u> scene, you're not--HUMANITARIAN.

Farrakhan. We don't have tea. I have met the Avidly Assaulted One once. About a quarter century ago, a woman poet, then a Muslim, brought him to meet my husband and myself. He was impressively relaxed. He brought no guards, no guns. We were impressed by his warm eyes, his kind patience, flexible dignity. He listened to our ideas. He listened to every word we said. He waited for us to finish our sentences. He never interrupted. (Today, interruption is an Art.) He did not feel the need to pastor. At least, he did not pastor. He did not ask us to join anything.

This man I have not seen since. He is, however, a member of Black Family. He is a Family Picture. I look at the picture. I don't want to forget that this individual has saved a lot of sick-souled, gasping, bare-footed Blacks no one else cared to save. He has fed them, medicated them, detoxicated them, schooled them: thus making many of <u>our</u> lives, homes and little children a SMIDGEN safer. Sometimes, where there is Mess, and he is called, Mess is stomped upon. He is not Malcolm. But do remember that <u>Malcolm</u> could be called, <u>would</u> come, would lift that one open hand, and -- Mirabile Dictu -- WONDERFUL to tell of -- Mess would be mesmerized and shorn.

Remember also Martin, Medgar, Fannie Lou, Ida B. Wells, Chicago's Haki, Jesse, Carol, California's Maxine, others, others. Without this Sweet Sentience -- the difficult strainings -- many of us who are still living would not be. We would be <u>missing,</u> or stiff in strict and restricted little lives. We should keep those names, and memories of what those names <u>meant</u>, and mean, as companions, richly with us as we walk our streets, breathing in our precious air, and symbolically spitting on a few of the Homeless. Those leaders, their acts, their influence, their belief in the power of affirming decency, keep many of the wild and beastified somewhat hopeful, willing to wait a little longer, willing to be watchful, willing to forswear those calm deliberate walks up aisles of trains or planes with guns a-blazing.

I Use them all. I appreciate all the Radiance.

But I must supplement.

I do not worship any Big Person. A long life has taught me that rigorous worship of Big Persons is not an intelligent management of my time. A long life has taught me that many of the Lit-tul people are large enough to merit my salute, my practical gratitude.

Middle-aged Martha Steward in a class at Chicago State University improves her classmates every Thursday night without once indicating that she considers herself superior to them in any way. No pastoring, but warmth, clear wit, bread-and-vegetables wisdom, kindness. (Kindness is not popular.)

A "word" about Big Persons:

I shall tell you a thing about giants
that you do not wish to know.
Giants look in mirrors and see
amost nothing at all.
But they leave their houses nevertheless.
They lurch out of doors --
to reach you, the other stretchers and
strainers.
(Erased under ermine or loud in tatters, oh
moneyed or mashed, you matter.
You matter, and giants must bother.)

Well, I shall not join the Muslims nor any other
Passionate Purity. But; instead of popping all these
pebbles at the Purposeful Pastor, why are we not
surveying with seriousness a mightily impressive and
altering tumor of our day? Vladimir Zhirinovsky hates
the idea of "all these Blacks" running around in this
country, with "all this Power." And the complete
population of the Jews, he opines, should settle in Israel.
(Isn't THAT resented?) He affirms Manifest Destiny,
believes that it was right to strip the Indians (I can't
remember his bothering to use the name Native
Americans) of most that was theirs. Zhirinovsky is
media-manager, hostility-heater, malevolent Player. Few
want to talk about him. Few admit Fear. I feel I'm back in
the late Thirties. I am not a social scientist, I am not a
fluent Politico. But when I look at Zhirinovsky I think of

John Donne's Bell. It tolls for Thee. "Never send to know
For Whom the Bell tolls. It tolls for THEE."

I am sure that one of Zhirinovsky's admirations is
Niccolo Machiavelli, author of "The Prince." Surely
Zhirinovsky squealed and dampened himself when he read
"A Prince should disregard the reproach of being thought
cruel where it enables him to keep his Subjects united and
obedient." Surely it was a while before Z was dry. And
likely he was again visited by difficulties when he went on
to read: "Fortune is a woman, who, to be kept under, must
be beaten and roughly handled; and we see that she suffers
herself to be more readily mastered by those who so
treat her than by those who are more timid in their
approaches."

What "awaits" The Black Community? It is a wide
community: that fact sometimes seems negligible, since
not all members flash their membership cards. The
community is seen in its True Strength, however, when
Union, obviously, is absolutely necessary, as it was when
Harold Washington decided to run for the mayorship of
Chicago. The Big Persons remembered that they, too, go
to the bathroom every day, if health permits, and joined
the workaday and the wee. All together came the proud
and the profane, the handsome, the homely, the spotty and
the spangled, the galloping and the halt, the wheeled and
the becrutched, the devilish and the demure. They grinned

at each other. They hollered "Here's Harold!" And they
put their Prince in a City Chair.

Is there a Decision? -- do Blacks need another Martin,
Malcolm, Medgar, Ida, Fannie Lou? Let's go back to looking
at those Littles. Their pictures overwhelm my Gallery. I
re-emphasize: perhaps what we need is not another
Individual to be roared up, royalized, routed -- but lots of
the Littles, understanding the strength of clean
cooperation, responsibility. From "Primer For Blacks:" I
go on believing that the Weak among us will, finally,
perceive the impressiveness of our numbers, perceive the
quality and legitimacy of our essence, and take sufficient,
indicated steps toward definition, clarification,
connection.

All Family Pictures looked at. With clean eyes.

There are no magics, no elves,
no timely godmothers to guide us.
We are lost, must wizard a track
through our own screaming weed.

An emphasis is paroled.
The old decapitations are revised,
the dispossessions beakless.

THEN we sing.
Note: The Jefferson Lecture; May 4, 1994; Kennedy Center Concert Hall,
Washington, D.C. Audience: 2,300.

"I'M HERE"

In Re: Beryl.

The country knows her.

She it is who tells me I've won the Aiken-Taylor Award, the American Book Award, the National Book Award Medal, the Essence Award, and at least half of seventy-plus Honorary Doctorate degrees. "They" call her to announce that I am to recite in tribute to Mayor Harold Washington at his First Inauguration, and at his Second Inauguration - requests of Chicago's first Black mayor.

She it is who sings through the wires: "The Frost Medal from The Poetry Society of America!" I hear, first from her, news of The National Endowment For The Arts Lifetime Achievement Award. (She makes me sit down to hear that it is accompanied by $40,000, my life's largest prize.) She is the one to tell me that I am the first, the only American to receive the Society For Literature Award, University of Thessaloniki, Athens, Greece. She makes me sit down to eat the feast-news that The National Endowment For The Humanities has chosen me as 1994 Jefferson Lecturer. "Listen to this!" (She's gurgling.) "Listen to the official description! -- 'the highest honor the Federal Government bestows for intellectual achievement in the Humanities'!" She tells me the news of a Gwendolyn Brooks Junior High School in Harvey, Illinois, of a Gwendolyn Brooks Elementary School in Aurora, of a Gwendolyn Brooks Cultural Center on the campus of Western Illinois University. My agent and my friend for about thirty years. Throughout those years, her cheery telephone theme has been "I'm Here."

I am using her theme to ribbonize people who, for long, have been "here" for me. Although I have hundreds of Friends (sometimes <u>strangers</u> become warm friends or "spiritual" associates), I want to *italicize* active and steady supports. Loyal and long-lasting supports. Excluding Family and excluding The Dead, here they are: *Haki Madhubuti (Don L. Lee) and his wife Safisha, Walter Bradford, Dudley Randall, Margaret Taylor Goss Burroughs, Richard and Jeanne Orlikoff (Dick Orlikoff,* my attorney for more than a quarter of a century), *Beryl and Gene Zitch, D.H. Melhem, Diana and Harry Mark Petrakis, Alice and Robert Cromie, Roy Lewis, Dr. Walter O. Evans of Detroit, Kenny Williams, Val Gray Ward and Francis Ward, Stephen Caldwell Wright, Gloria and Lerone Bennett, Cynthia Walls, Edward Richardson, Brenda and Trent Malone, Dolores Kendrick, Ann Smith, Mari Evans.*

AFTERWORD

D.H. MELHEM

In 1968, Gwendolyn Brooks was already a poet with a national reputation. She was the new Poet Laureate of Illinois, succeeding the late Carl Sandburg. She had won a Pulitzer Prize for poetry in 1950 for *Annie Allen*, would soon be nominated for a National Book Award in 1969 for *In the Mecca*, and, at age fifty-one, could look ahead to a comfortable niche on her publisher's list. Instead, she turned to Dudley Randall's nascent Broadside Press, started her own magazine, *The Black Position*, and embarked on a journey of commitment that continues to this day.

It is helpful to place these facts in a historical context, to recall that Martin Luther King, Jr., was assassinated in the year that also saw the murder of Robert F. Kennedy, that it was a rebellious decade of riots and Vietnam War protests that intensified the clamorous mounting of the Civil Rights movement. Brooks's biographer, the late George E. Kent, wrote: "Gwendolyn Brooks shares with Langston Hughes the achievement of being responsive to turbulent changes in the Black community's vision of itself and to the changing forms of its vibrations during decades of rapid change." What springs replenish the vigor of her integrity?

The sources begin in a nurturing home environment. Gwendolyn Brooks, who was to become the consummate Chicagoan, was born in Topeka, Kansas, at the home of her maternal grandparents. She entered the world on June 7, 1917, the first child of "duty-loving" Keziah Wims Brooks, a fifth-grade teacher in Topeka, who played the piano and wrote music, and David Anderson Brooks, son of a runaway slave, a janitor with "rich Artistic Abilities" who had spent a year at Fisk University in Nashville. After five weeks she and her mother returned to Chicago. Sixteen months after her own birth, her brother Raymond was born.

Brooks showed early signs of literary prodigy, and she grew up in an atmosphere where she was encouraged and appreciated. The child wrote in notebooks, rhyming from the age of seven and casting her thoughts into didactic and soaring verse about nature, love, death, and the sky. Like Maud Martha, heroine of her novel, she would sit on the back steps of her house and dream, searching the clouds, conceiving her rhymes. Her mother told her, "You are going to be the *lady* Paul Laurence Dunbar."

Reared in a Black neighborhood from the age of four, "semi-poor," as she describes the family circumstances, by eleven the precocious writer had four poems published locally in the *Hyde Parker*, by thirteen she was published in *American Childhood*; by sixteen she had become a weekly contributor to the *Chicago Defender* column "Lights and Shadows," where seventy-five of her poems were printed within two years.

Brooks's emphasis on what she calls "Familyhood" for Blacks extends her personal recognition to its social value. "I had always felt that to be Black was good," she writes in her autobiography, *Report From Part One (1972)*. Her work indicates an indomitable ego strength and a dedication whose roots are fed, as Kent points out, by a "religious consciousness, from which dogma has been ground away." Brooks herself says, "My religion is . . . PEOPLE. LIVING," and she has often remarked, "My religion is kindness." Church, nevertheless, provided a cultural nexus. The Black heritage of music was maintained by her father, who often sang, and by her pianist mother. Mrs. Brooks, who taught Sunday school, encouraged her daughter to write plays for her pupils; performers included the young writer. Church was the repository of Black oratory and the spirituals that W.E.B. DuBois in *The Gift of Black Folk* called "sorrow songs." It was the place where the poet's mother took her to meet James Weldon Johnson and Langston Hughes. The latter became an inspiration, and, later, a friend.

On September 17, 1939, Brooks was married to Henry L. Blakely II, a poet and writer whom she had met in a youth group sponsored by the National Association for the Advancement of Colored People (NAACP). On October 10, 1940, her son Henry Jr. was born. On September 8, 1951, daughter Nora was born. Brooks was proud of her children and of her childbearing; her body had performed as it was "*supposed* to perform."

Early publishing also increased the confidence of the young poet. At first she seemed, according to Elizabeth Lawrence, her longtime editor at Harper and Brothers (now HarperCollins), suited to addressing smaller audiences; the impression soon vanished. The warm critical reception of *A Street in Bronzeville* (1945), her first book, helped to sustain her growth as a public figure.

Brooks lived the Black experience in the United States. While fostering rare encouragement by a few teachers, school brought an awakening to the discriminatory nature of the intra- and interracial scene. As a dark-skinned child, as a woman, Brooks learned first-hand the valuing of whiteness and lightness, transferred from the dominant culture to prejudices among Blacks themselves. The awareness figures in her earlier work and in her novel, *Maud Martha*. Upon graduation from Wilson Junior College (now Kennedy-King), at first the only work the poet could find was that of a domestic. Later, she worked as a writer and make-up assistant for *The Women's National Magazine*. Then, in the Mecca Building, a formerly grand apartment complex that had deteriorated into a slum dwelling, she worked for four "horrible" months as secretary to a spiritual adviser who sold lucky numbers and "magic potions." Impressions from the indelible experience vivify the setting of *In the Mecca*, recalling Brooks's invocation of Walt Whitman's literary summons to "vivify the contemporary fact."

At any period, a survey of Brooks's works will yield her dominant social concerns, ranging from war and peace, the Civil Rights movement, the Black Rebellion, a sense of African heritage, and the welfare of women and children, to the need for courage and Resistance. Soren Kierkegaard's dictum, "Purity of heart is to will one thing," applies here. For Brooks, that underlying, coherent impulse is *caritas*, nourished by a sense of African identity and a vivid sense of the Black Nation as an extension of the Black family. Caritas translates Brooks's humane vision into a heroic voice, one bearing its own prosodic strength and articulating the needs of the Black community for pride, liberty, and leadership.

Those major themes distinctly register in Brooks's first book, *A Street in Bronzeville*, which offers a series of vignettes and interpretations of Black life. The poet counterpoints her humane conceptions of the entrapments of daily existence with memorable portraits: "Negro Hero," "The Sundays of Satin-Legs Smith," "Ballad of Pearl May Lee," "Queen of the Blues," and "Hattie Scott." She confronts what Arthur P. Davis refers to as the "black-and-tan" motif in her work, i.e., the valuing of lightness above darkness. The book demonstrates Brooks's comprehensive sensibility and technical skill (see especially the antiwar sonnet sequence "Gay Chaps at the Bar"), and her social identity. Like Langston Hughes, she is able to adapt conventional forms on her way to developing the new.

Annie Allen (1949), Brooks's antiromantic poem sequence about a young Black woman's prewar illusions and post-war realities, again identifies the pressures of daily life. The centerpiece is "The Anniad," its mock heroic second section; the closing "Womanhood" poems begin with a brilliant sonnet sequence, "the children of the poor," and portray a brave, yet circumspect Annie, impelled by motherhood, who looks out from her own problems toward a world she would like to reform. Her psychic growth and sturdy triumph inspired poet Nikki Giovanni to recognize Annie as "my mother."

The manuscript history of Maud Martha (1953), with its metamorphoses and revisions, attests to the poet's perseverance. An unpretentious masterpiece, this impressionistic bildungsroman retains an episodic structure that would lend itself to film. In recent years it has been given critical attention, particularly by Black feminists. Themes of "Black-and-tan," Black-and-white, economic hardship, female dependence, and muted and outright defiance lattice the personal narrative.

The Bean Eaters (1960) sounds the righteous thunder of the Civil Rights movement. Regarding the book's mixed reception, due to her "forsaking lyricism for polemics," Brooks observed years later in a *Black Books Bulletin* interview with Haki R. Madhubuti (then don l. lee), "To be Black is political." She further noted, in a marginal comment to me on my *Gwendolyn Brooks* manuscript, "Of course, to be *any*thing in this world as it is 'socially' constructed, is 'political.' "The book's challenging current topics include school integration in Little Rock, Arkansas, housing integration, the lynching of Emmett Till in Mississippi, Black pride, and the needs of women and children. *Selected Poems* (1963) includes new works, among them "Riders to the Blood-red Wrath," a tribute to the Freedom Riders, and their "canny consorts."

In 1967, at the Second Fisk University Writers' Conference in Nashville, Brooks met the artistic resonance of the Black Rebellion: the Black Arts Movement and its founder, Amiri Baraka (then LeRoi Jones). Although Brooks's work had always been vitally focused, the experience she describes in her autobiography resembles an epiphany, comparable to Wordsworth's on Mount Snowdon in *The Prelude* (Book XIV), or Alfred's on the balcony in "*In The Mecca*." Upon returning home, she started a workshop for the Blackstone Rangers, a teenaged Chicago gang, and gave Dudley Randall permission to publish "The Wall" as a broadside. The following year, he published the memorial broadside, "Martin Luther King,

Jr.," written on April 4, the day of the assassination, and appearing April 5 on the front page of the *Chicago Sun-Times.*

In the Mecca (1968) became her "brief epic" (as John Milton referred to *Paradise Regain'd*). Her jacket statement reads, "I was to be a Watchful Eye, a Tuned Ear, a Super-Reporter." The Super-Reporter, whom Brooks conceives as one who is "just supremely *accurate,*" suggests quasi-divine reportage, the quest foreshadowed in the need for a "Teller" in "One wants a Teller in a time like this" (*Annie Allen*), and the prophetic role confirmed in later works, such as "In Montgomery" (1971), the major piece that introduces "verse journalism." "In The Mecca", Brooks's longest single work in the book, recounts the tragic search of a mother for her child. The woman's frantic pilgrimage through the building reveals a failed socioeconomic system, a failed art, a failed religion, and their spawn of isolation and rage. A want of caritas, Brooks's major theme, mirrors deficiencies of the white environment and reflects the Mecca as a microcosm. The multiple embedding of poetic forms and their orchestration open freely to content and convey a liberation. The poet calls for a "new art and anthem" that will redeem grief with, as expressed by one of her characters, "an essential sanity, black and electric."

The epilogic poems of "After Mecca" offer tributes, hope, and direction. The two "Sermon(s) on the Warpland" proclaim her "grand heroic" style (to borrow a modifier from Matthew Arnold), as distinguished from the "plain heroic" of some later works, and adapt the sermon, particularly in the changed genre, as an art form. As a stylistic term, "grand heroic" indicates use of imperatives, parallel constructions, redundant phrasing, metaphor and metonymy, and biblical modes. From the sonnet, Brooks advances to a "tom-tom hearted" present. "My people, Black and Black, revile the River. / Say that the River turns, and turn the River." counsels the First Sermon. The Second Sermon commands, "This is the urgency:Live!. . .Conduct your blooming in the noise and whip of the whirlwind."

After *In The Mecca*, Brooks aimed to support the Black press. Several companies published her work; she contributed financially to them. Dudley Randall's Broadside Press published *Riot* (1969), *Family Pictures* (1970), *Aloneness* (1971), *Report from Part One* (1972), and *Beckonings* (1975); Haki R. Madhubuti's Third World Press *published The Tiger Who Wore White Gloves* (1974) and *To Disembark* (1981). In the eighties she settled on The David Company, named after her late father, and began publishing her own works: *Primer for Blacks* and *Young Poet's Primer* (1980), *Very Young Poets* (1983); *The Near-Johannesburg Boy and Other Poems* (1986); *Gottschalk and the Grand Tarantelle* (1988). With *Blacks* (1987), she put her unavailable works back into print. Her publishing gesture was as feminist as it was Black, bespeaking dignity and emancipation. She has recently resumed publishing with Madhubuti's Third World Press, which has reissued *Blacks, Maud Martha*, and five other works, but the poet retains her prerogative to bring out some of her own poetry, and has done so *with Children Coming Home* (1991). Her itinerary of readings and workshops, arranged by her agent and friend Beryl Zitch, director of The Contemporary Forum, continues unabated. The poet has also traveled to Ghana, Kenya, and Tanzania in Africa, and to England, France, Russia, and Canada.

My first attendance at a Brooks reading took place in 1971 at the City College of New York, where she was teaching as a distinguished professor of the arts. A current of excitement preceded her arrival; when she appeared, she received a standing ovation. People responded to whatever she read or said; a kind of dialogue was in progress, almost as if a brilliant friend - or mother! - had come to visit students at their school. What I heard, moreover, in her musical cadences was a spiritual and prosodic power, a poetry of humane vision and leadership. With meticulous aptness it combined the energy of African drums, the rhythms of Black music, its blues and jazz, the Black sermon, the Anglo-Saxon alliterative poetic, the ballad, and the sonnet, and forged something new. Later on I would account the presences of Walt Whitman and Emily Dickinson, a comprehension of modern poetry from Langston Hughes to Robert Frost, Edna St. Vincent Millay, and T.S. Eliot. As Brooks herself says: "The Black poet has the 'American' experience and also has the Black experience; so is very rich." And while addressing herself primarily to Blacks, she insists, "I know that the Black emphasis must be, not *against white*, but FOR *Black*." She has left the sometimes elliptical mode of earlier work for one that she calls "clarifying, not simple." Aiming to "call" Black people to unity and pride, she has raised the communicative power of poetry to the rhetoric of music.

Although in 1968 James N. Johnson, reviewing *In the Mecca* for *Ramparts*, wrote, "No white poet of her quality is so undervalued, so unpardonably unread," and the *New York Times* last reviewed one of her books in February 1973 (Toni Cade Bambara's excellent piece on *Report from Part One*), Brooks has become the most widely honored poet in the United States. When in 1974 I began my study of her work, there was not a single volume about her; now there are several, in addition to a proliferation of essays and her numerous appearances in anthologies. She is the first Black to win a Pulitzer Prize of any kind. Indeed, until its conferral in May 1950, no Black had won any of the significant awards of our time. There had been no Black Drama Critics' Circle Award, no Black National Book Award, no Black Nobel Prize. (Ralph Bunche received the Peace Prize in June of 1950). Brooks has received two Guggenheim fellowships, an American Academy of Arts and Letters Award in literature, and the first Kuumba Liberation Award. She was the first Black woman to receive the Shelley Memorial Award and the Frost Medal of the Poetry Society of America. She was the first Black woman to be appointed Consultant in Poetry to the Library of Congress, and the last to be so designated before the title was changed to Poet Laureate (and was granted to Robert Penn Warren); and also first to be elected to the National Institute of Arts and Letters, (thirty-two years after the election of W.E.B. DuBois, the first Black).

Inducted into the National Women's Hall of Fame in 1988, in the same year she was notified of a Senior Fellowship in Literature grant from the National Endowment for the Arts in recognition, as an official put it, of "the spirit of the work and life of the author." She has more than seventy honorary doctorates.

In the tradition of her youthful experience in which poor strangers were fed at the family table, Brooks's generosity is legendary. As Poet Laureate of Illinois, she established annual Poet Laureate Awards (this year will be their twenty-seventh anniversary), primarily for the elementary and high school students of Illinois. She continually endows many other prizes. Encouraging writing in schools, in prisons, in her vicinity, and wherever she travels, she has probably done more than anyone to promote the writing of poetry throughout the United States.

Brooks's oeuvre reflects her concern with the young. Poems such as the famous "We Real Cool" in The Bean Eaters and Boys. Black in Beckonings, books such as Bronzeville Boys and Girls, The Tiger Who Wore White Gloves, Young Poet's Primer, Very Young Poets, and Children Coming Home attest to her involvement. More than mere objects of sentiment, children embody the future, which for Brooks incorporates present responsibilities. And yet the span from Bronzeville Boys and Girls (1956) to Children Coming Home is less a bridge than a chasm; the contrast is harsh. The Watchful Eye, caring yet unflinching, sees today's children in their context, and the vision itself proclaims an emergency. Yet throughout her work, as in person, Brooks's wry humor and lively sense of life's absurdities fuel her optimism. Remedies are possible; she believes in growth and change at any age. The adage "When handed a lemon, make lemonade" is one of her favored "life-lines."

In her closeness and accessibility to common life, poet and person seamlessly coincide. Not since the Fireside Poets of the American Civil War has one inspired so much personal affection. Having influenced, assisted, and supported the work of writers in and out of her workshops - one can only begin the distinguished list with Haki R. Madhubuti, Carolyn M. Rodgers, and the late Etheridge Knight - she is the subject of two tribute anthologies, To Gwen With Love (1971) and Say That The River Turns: The Impact of Gwendolyn Brooks (1987).

Conferences at Colorado State and Chicago State Universities have been devoted to her work. A Gwendolyn Brooks Cultural Center has been founded at Western Illinois University; a junior high school was named for her in Harvey, Illinois; and an elementary school in Aurora, Illinois. Chicago State University, where she retains a Chair (a professorship named in her honor) houses the Gwendolyn Brooks Center for Black Literature and Creative Writing.

In 1821, Thomas De Quincey wrote of the "Literature of Knowledge and Literature of Power": The function of the first was to teach, of the second, to move. He compared the former to a rudder, the latter, to an oar or sail, stirring the reader "to the higher understanding or reason, but always through affections of pleasure and sympathy." A fine recent poem epitomizes Brooks's ability to animate the reader/listener's sympathetic understanding. In "An Old Black Woman, Homeless and Indistinct," having described how "Your every day is a pilgrimage. / A blue hubbub," and what it is like to face the street, "your incessant enemy," avoided by passers-by, like the rich girl who "sees you not, who sees you very well," Brooks concludes:

Black old woman, homeless, indistinct -
Your last and least adventure is Review.
Folks used to celebrate your birthday!
Folks used to say "She's such a pretty little thing!"

Folks used to say "She draws such handsome
                                horses, cows and houses."
Folks used to say "That child is going far."

These humble references image the tragic essence of
life, the losses that nibble away at time and its core of
hope. Often, as she does here, Brooks combines the
literature of knowledge with the literature of power. She
fulfills the office of Teacher, as William Wordsworth
respectfully capitalized the word, and Dudley Randall
acknowledged in his tribute "For Gwendolyn Brooks,
Teacher." Instructing the sensibility, her heart shares
its illuminations. Her poems present "an essential sanity,
black and electric." While our time of social laxity and
malaise narrows its band of exemplary figures, the ideals
of virtue and communality diminish into wistful exchanges
with the past. And so we welcome this major voice that
affirms in "Paul Robeson." "We are each other's
business. / We are each other's magnitude and bond."
Brooks is our national resource, our finest ore.

Note1 - "An Old Black Woman, Homeless and Indistinct," ©1993 by
Gwendolyn Brooks. Quoted by permission - Drumvoices Revue,
(Fall-Winter 1992/1993), p.120. Note 2 - D.H. Melhem, poet,
critic, and novelist, is the author of Gwendolyn Brooks: Poetry and
the Heroic Voice and Heroism in the New Black Poetry. In 1980
Melhem received a National Endowment for the Humanities
fellowship. The above appreciation, substantially as it appears, was
first published in the Jefferson Lecture issue of Humanities - 1994.

APPENDIX

APPENDIX

HENRY L. BLAKELY II

Find a full portrait of my husband in "Report From Part One," but I want to add: _____

It is not to be forgotten that my husband, proud Black man (and author of "Windy Place"), <u>did</u> say, pre– and post–wedding, that my writing was more important than impeccable housework — that I must never sacrifice my writing for sweeping, cooking, or washing the dishes.

He has always been delighted when honors have been accorded me. Always sparkles when I tell him What Has Happened! Almost inevitably he will say "How happy your mother, your father would be!" He loved my parents, David and Keziah — loved to be with them. The affection was reciprocated; moreover, they respected him and admired him genuinely, and felt that he was exactly the "right husband" for their daughter. My mother especially appreciated the fact that he loved taking me "places," both before and after marriage.

September 17, 1995, will see our Fifty-Sixth anniversary.

HENRY L. BLAKELY III

As a child, always a distinguished little scientist, always brightly technological.

Grew up to be a California software designer, aggressively creative, husband to Lillian, a computer expert, and father to Nicholas, now seven, and already a self-possessed computer expert.

But here again (pulled out of "Report From Part One") is his Portrait Pre-eminent:

Henry of the Thousand Good-nights

Have you seen him at Christmas? Have you seen him at Easter?

At Christmas compare him to the Christmas tree. He is like the boiling in the bubbling–lights. You know that gentle boiling. He makes Santa Clauses, and throws the tinsel icicles up in the Christmas tree. And he gives gifts. Claps his hands and whistles.

At Easter he is a shining little boy in his new navy blue or tan or grayish suit, and his new hat that is almost like a man's. When church–time comes, he takes Mama's arm, helping her through the happenchance of the street.

And of all the voices climbing to the high dome of the temple, his is the loudest and the most holy.

You have not seen him at night, when he has two hundred good-nights for each beloved soul, including that of Cocoa, his puppy and that of Water Boy, his fish. "Good-night! Good-night! Good-night!" Every night the chorus rings through the house, until the Old Heads are ready to burst. "Good-night! Good-night! Good-night." Just before pajama-time. At pajama-time. Before prayer-time. After prayer-time. At getting-in-bed time. After getting-in-bed time. At lights-out music.

There's Henry. The one run–walking. The one skip–hopping. The one bounce–jumping. Spring flowers are in his fist. "My goodness!" says Mama. "Flowers!"

"Tulips," says Henry. "These red ones come from Mrs. Tubbs'. These purple ones come from Mrs. Smith's. These yellow ones come from Mrs. Allison's. They are all for you."

Mama is not sure.

"Do you mean that Mrs. Tubbs and Mrs. Smith and Mrs. Allison all sent these pretty flowers just for me?"

There is silence.

Do Mrs. Tubbs and Mrs. Smith and Mrs. Allison know that I am getting these pretty flowers?"

There is silence.

Now Mama is making I'm–sorry calls on the telephone.

Now Henry is standing in a corner with his face to the wall, and his hands folded neatly behind him.

NORA BROOKS BLAKELY

From the moment of her birth she was a lovely, loving radiance, a sparkling child. She grew up to be my best friend. She grew up to be an educator, then founder and director of a Chicago children's theatre, Chocolate Chips Theatre Company.

We send notes to each other, we send full–blown letters, we talk to each other on the telephone for a minute, twelve minutes, half an hour, four hours. We advise each other, we correct each other, we scold or semi–scold each other, we praise and honor each other.

Here's "Mama" on the telephone to Nora, in re a TV fright movie ("IT") which she had mischievously urged me to see, playing down its tummy–tousling horror: "OK — you tried to have "fun" wit' Mama: Mama told you there would be a cemetery in "IT": and you said "NAY." Well, dear daughter, I turned on "IT", and immediately there was this cemetery scene with a small clown much in need of dental work. Thanks, kid."

When my mother died on March 14, 1978, two weeks after her ninetieth birthday, my daughter was a rich support. I have always regretted that I was not at my mother's bedside at the moment she died. I was out of town that day, but Nora came, and spent a lovely time with Keziah and our all–day nurse on that Last Day Alive.

I was on a train, enroute home. Nora called me on the train. The conductor stopped the train, and accompanied me to a telephone in a tiny railroad station Somewhere. I called Nora, got the News. I went back to Chicago by plane. What a comfort was that Daughter — in the most traumatic time of my life. Subsequently, she was always available for those talks which, to the bereaved, mean more than bread and water, more than head-pats and consolation–hugs. Nora wrote a sensitive poem to which I can refer when I need the nourishment it inevitably provides. A very This–Is–For–<u>Our</u>–Family poem. It's addressed to me.

FOR MAMA

Red gold dances through our minds
whirling up thoughts of Other who <u>is</u> still here.
Memories make lives livable again.
Memories call learnings and giggles galore.
Yes — and flashes of hot pain
      and stopsoul sorrow, too
           but
           <u>she</u> lives
and chuckles and "pshaws" away —
As long as we light love candles of thought and times-
                              when,
as long as our regrettings are syncopated sadnesses
              with a happy beat

as long as you are of she
                    and all are in me
and we laugh, and we straighten
and root ourselves
                    in the Here.

Nora Brooks Blakely

Today's media narratives, featuring woeful relations between mothers and daughters, alarm us. They make us proud to call attention to a very different kind of story.

Gwendolyn Brooks, the first Black to win a Pulitzer Prize of any kind (1950), was born in Topeka, Kansas, June 7, 1917, and has lived in Chicago, Illinois since she was a few weeks old. She is a graduate of Chicago's Wilson Junior College, and has been awarded over seventy honorary degrees. She has taught at the University of Wisconsin (Madison), City College of New York, Columbia College of Chicago, Northeastern Illinois University, Elmhurst College, Chicago State University. Since 1968 she has been Poet Laureate of Illinois, succeeding the first Poet Laureate, Carl Sandburg. In 1988 she was inducted into the National Women's Hall of Fame. She has published many books, including poetry for adults and children, one novel, writing manuals, an autobiography.

In 1985 she became the 29th and final appointment as Consultant in Poetry to the Library of Congress. She is a member of the American Academy and Institute of Arts and Letters. Among her awards are: the American Academy of Arts and Letters Award, the Shelley Memorial Award, the Ainsfield-Wolf Award, the Kuumba Liberation Award, two Guggenheim Fellowships, the Frost Medal from the Poetry Society of America, a National Book Award nomination for "In the Mecca," the National Endowment for The Arts Lifetime Achievement Award in 1989. She is the only American to receive the Society for Literature Award, University of Thessaloniki, Athens, Greece (1990). She is a Jefferson Lecturer, 1994, and National Book Awards Medalist For Distinguished Contribution To American Letters, 1994. She is also winner of The Sewanee Review's Aiken-Taylor Award, the sixth recipient. October 5, 1995: the National Medal of Arts (at the White House).

In Illinois, she has enjoyed many special honors: in Harvey, there is the Gwendolyn Brooks Junior High School; on the campus of Western Illinois University in Macomb there is the Gwendolyn Brooks Cultural Center; in Chicago's Cabrini Green community, the Edward Jenner School auditorium has been named after her; and her name has been engraved on the Illinois State Library in Springfield.

She is the daughter of the late David and Keziah (Wims) Brooks. She is married to Henry Blakely, author of "Windy Place," and is the mother of Nora Brooks Blakely, founder and director of Chocolate Chips Theatre Company in Chicago, and Henry Blakely, Jr., a California software designer.